Conversational Intelligence® @Work

Build Trust, Culture & Performance

A book dedicated to the work of Judith E. Glaser

by the C-IQ West Coast Mastermind

Banning · Curtin · Gleason
Mitchell · Stevenson · Underhill

This publication is designed to provide practical examples and applications of the principles embodying Conversational Intelligence® (C-IQ). This is a book about transforming conversations and results with sophistication and mastery.

Published in ©MMXXIII by the C-IQ West Coast Mastermind, the book is a collaborative effort between book whisperer Timi Gleason and co-authors: Rickie Banning, Susan Curtin, Gwen Mitchell, Sue Stevenson, and Dave Underhill. The book is published by Willow Creek Publishing.

Excerpt rights are granted and encouraged with the following wording: Conversational Intelligence® @Work by the C-IQ West Coast Mastermind.

For information on speaking, coaching or consulting, please contact the individual authors using the contact information at the end of the book, or on LinkedIn.

For reprint rights, contact: TimiGleason@WillowCreekPublishing.store

V1.0
ISBN paperback 978-0-9843275-1-5
Printed in the United States of America

About Willow Creek Publishing Store

Willow Creek Publishing Store is a book publishing and on-line distribution company for business education and business-themed "how to" books dealing with coaching, strategic management, communications, career and legacy planning, and topics of professional development.

A Tribute to Judith E. Glaser
by the C-IQ West Coast Mastermind

Jun 23, 1946 to Nov 18, 2018

Judith E. Glaser was a powerful mentor and teacher, and a very generous soul. She understood how to break down a conversation and ensure it hit its mark. She left us with key conversational distinctions so anyone who wanted to, could learn how to heal their communications and relationships.

Judith role-modeled Listening to Connect and Double Clicking. She was prolific, authentic, and generous. She wanted ALL OF US to be successful.

As certified graduates of her courses and teachings, the West Coast Mastermind strives to embody Conversational Intelligence® (C-IQ) as Judith intended. In her memory, we have pooled our collective knowledge and experiences to share with our readers the richness of Judith's legacy.

In German, to create a book that honors a respected person is to create a "Festschrift."

Judith, this is your festschrift from us. Thank you for the extensive body of work that you have left behind to guide us masterfully and intentionally through our conversations.

Table of Contents

Part I: Setting the Stage: The C-IQ Mindset

The Cat is Out of The Bag (*Timi Gleason*) 1

Conversational NeuroPerspectives
(*Sue Stevenson*)... 5

Conversing With The Elephant in The Room
(*Gwen Mitchell*) ………………………………………21

Realizing It's An Inside Job (*Rickie Banning*) ...…….43

Part II: Conversations: Large and Small

How to Develop and Provide Trust in Teams
(*Susan Curtin*) 81

Conversations That Build Trust and Inspire
(*Dave Underhill*) .... ……………………………...113

C-IQ Coach-Author Profiles 131

Part I: Setting the Stage:
The C-IQ Mindset

How is Conversational Intelligence® (C-IQ) so transformative? It seems to captivate our hearts and minds in unsuspecting ways with its three Levels. It has Blind Spots. There are Essentials. And it can be magical.

In this book, we will be exploring the practical magic of Conversational Intelligence®, the life work of thought-leader and educator Judith E. Glaser and her teachings.

Perhaps you have already read Judith's book *Conversational Intelligence®, How Great Leaders Build Trust and Get Extraordinary Results*. Or you may have been fortunate enough to attend her classes and certification courses between 2016-2018, as we did.

Like learning a foreign language, we desire to express our new vocabulary and wisdom within our daily lives. But what does that look like? Judith's book leaves us inspired but wondering what it is like in the real world? How are others applying the principles in their jobs and outside work? Embodying Conversational Intelligence® can, at first, feel awkward.

Our journey starts with an overview of how essential Conversational Intelligence® knowledge and techniques are translating in this post-pandemic world. Whether we knew the cultural shifts were coming or not, our economy, social lives, health practices, and our workplaces have experienced unexpected changes. Socially we have had to proceed without new ground rules, or the benefit of previous experience. But those of us who know C-IQ have been able to draw on strong foundations for communicating in any situation, and this has helped us in many ways to navigate new paths.

There are two parts to this book. In Part I, Sue Stevenson's chapter on the neuroscience of conversations and explores the role the brain plays in the mental and emotional triggers of daily life. You've possibly never pondered all the many neural transactions racing back and forth between your heart and your brain during your day. As our neurons are inundated at lightning speed with new situations and managing frustrations, we may feel we have limited choice over the outcomes of our inner workings; these neurological transactions are performed so miraculously and automatically by our bodies. How can we choose a path towards mastery and reduce the stress?

Conversational Intelligence® offers us the tools to manage ourselves and help others to master themselves. Sue demonstrates how C-IQ is built to honor and calm the activities and reactions of our brains and heart.

Then we move to Gwen Mitchell's chapter on the hidden dynamics behind our communications. With valuable stories, Gwen shows us how to become more aware of our blind spots in conversations so we can align our thoughts with our words and intentions.

Rickie Banning's thoughtful and optimistic stories are next. Rickie has extensive psychological background and experience coaching military personnel through their stress levels. Rickie illustrates how to use C-IQ techniques to build upon productive conversations.

Once you reach Part II, you will see the discussion shift to an exploration of Conversational Intelligence® in team dynamics, and in our last chapter, we will be examining the importance of how leaders develop conversations that build trust and inspire others to follow.

After reading these stories, you may become interested in studying to be a practitioner. Judith's company, The CreatingWE® Institute teaches, and annually, certifies individuals and their companies in Conversational Intelligence®. Website: CreatingWE.com.

For consulting assistance or coaching, you are invited to reach out to the authors who will be able to customize a solution for you. Information about the authors and the West Coast Mastermind Group are located at the back of the book.

The Cat Is Out of The Bag

~ Timi Gleason

"To get to the next level of greatness depends on the quality of the culture, which depends on the quality of the relationships, which depends on the quality of the conversations. Everything happens through conversations!"
~ Judith E. Glaser

If you've ever tried to catch a cat, it's not a straightforward task. In fact, it can be a very challenging experience for both you and the cat.

Usually, what makes it all the more difficult is that there's some kind of time pressure that requires you to catch the cat under duress instead of gently removing it while it's sitting in your lap. And as cats would have it, cats sense the incoming change and try to run from any compliance and from being caught. And yet, if you two worked together for a higher good, life would be much easier for you both.

During the pandemics, quarantines, and a multitude of sacrifices, it seems like almost everything familiar to our society changed in one form or another. These days:

- We may accomplish our work differently.
- We may have changed our sense of security in crowds and groups, including our work teams.
- And our abilities to meet safely in person are too frequently redefined by new, involuntary solutions.

Should we have to impose another quarantine anytime soon, it would not be easy for anyone to comply after all that we have sacrificed. Globally it's fair to say that many of us are fed up with requests for compliance and going-without! We have become like loose cats. We want nothing to do with more restrictions. And more than ever, we need the tools for working out our feelings through effective conversations.

So where do a country and a global workforce, battered by losses and extreme social changes, start? How will we agree on anything? How will we mutually redefine any sort of normalcy?

New solutions, approaches, and insights are greatly needed. The ability to be in conversation and in exploration with each other is critical. We see Conversational Intelligence® as an essential tool for co-creating our futures.

Like cats, we are part of a dynamic group. Our group is trying to come together under old agreements that need updates and fresh discussion! We must be willing to set aside the time necessary to authentically explore our needs and mutual goals with each other.

With C-IQ skills and knowledge, we can heal the past and powerfully step into our future. Not just at work but in politics, entertainment, tourism, health, and most importantly, our families.

In this book, we have shared our collective C-IQ experiences from inside this uniquely potent skillset. C-IQ is a bag of tools and attitude shifts that is rooted in neuroscience, Emotional Intelligence, and healthy team dynamics.

Its secret sauce is the willingness to take the time to become masterful communicators.

Conversational
NeuroPerspectives
  ~ Sue Stevenson

"Neurotransmitters are to the brain, what conversations are to relationships."

~ Judith E. Glaser

A Story: "Just Grunt!" What??

A subtle but important tip I learned early in my corporate career from a large HR conference speaker was about 'The Grunt.'

Little did I know that this tip would help open some improved communication and connections in my corporate role.

Allan Pease, an Australian body language expert and author, described how men and women show they are listening to one another. "...men use a series of short 'humphs' with an occasional nod of the head to show they are listening, which can be misinterpreted by women."

His advice to the women in the meeting when listening to the men was to sit expressionlessly, nod, grunt, and not interrupt. He observed that women who use this technique scored big points on the credibility scale from men.

When I experimented with grunting, I was surprised to find that my male colleagues were much more receptive to my ideas and contributions in meetings.

I became a pretty good grunter. I even got a bump up on my communication competency rating from my boss.

This is explained quite simply because men and women use a different range of high and low-pitched listening sounds, whereas men have a more restricted range.

The men have "difficulty decoding the meanings behind pitch changes, so they speak in a more monotone voice."

Perhaps "The Grunt" should be added to the communication skills curriculum taught at school.

In This Chapter

Was this all it took to improve the quality of conversations? Listen or observe the cues or expressions of my audience? No, it takes a lot more to truly understand our brain's role in Conversational Intelligence®, although actively listening is fundamental. In this chapter, I will outline some of the key elements we have gleaned from neuroscience and positive psychology that can be applied to how we have better conversations. The field of Conversational Intelligence®, which was developed by Judith E. Glaser, has opened up new perspectives and ideas about the quality of our conversations. My approach, which I call neuroperspectives, will examine conversations with the brain in mind that is told through stories, science, and possibly new ways of thinking and fresh perspectives.

Physical Threats and Neurochemistry

When we experience a threat response, such as interpreting movement in the bushes as a snake when it is just the wind, resources in the brain move away from the prefrontal cortex and into other parts of the body, so we can be prepared to run or attack. We need a greater level of blood flow to our arms and legs to run or fight, so the body redirects this oxygen-rich blood away from our brain. Our neurochemical balance also changes, and both cortisol and adrenaline flood our systems to help in our fight, flight or, sometimes, freeze response.

Have you ever been in a plane cockpit and observed how the emergency controls are directly in front of the pilot? This is to enable them to put into place the emergency drills they practiced automatically without wasting energy looking to the side or using peripheral vision. In an emergency situation or when other threats occur mid-flight, their vision narrows, and they can focus on what is right in front of them.

You may have heard this called the Amygdala hijack; however, I like to describe the response as the activation of the limbic circuitry combined with changes in our brain chemistry. We can see a dimming of our executive functions in the prefrontal cortex and a heightening of other capabilities that help us survive. Due to our redirection of resources, our peripheral vision, our digestive system, and even our use of logic are all reduced until the threat has passed or our perception of the threat has passed.

Social Threat

Our modern-day threats are more often social than physical ones described above. They are constant and varied but produce physical responses similarly. For example, I have observed many executives – myself included – who, under acute or chronic stress, can become overly narrowly focused on their tasks due to reduced peripheral vision. Their ability to see more widely and see the big picture is no longer available to them. This negatively impacts their creativity, open-mindedness, and communication ability, especially when trying to have a Level III or co-creating conversation. To learn more about the differences between Level I, II and III Conversations, please see the descriptions that Gwen Mitchell has provided in her chapter: *Conversing with the Elephant in the Room*. The ability to toggle between these three conversational levels provides extraordinary access to mastering complex communications.

We will hear from Rickie Banning in her chapter, *Realizing It's An Inside Job*, that "our brain is programmed to discern friend or foe, intuitively asking 'Is it safe or is there danger here?' We are always scanning the environment for threats - in fact, we scan for threats three to five times per second! When conversing with others, we ascertain whether the person is a friend or foe, whether we trust them or not. The threat we experience when there is a lack of trust has most of the characteristics that we experience with physical threats described above and does not serve us in building a relationship and communicating effectively.

The Social Brain and Social Pain

According to *Psychology Today*, "Largely, the social brain generally refers to the temporal-parietal junction, posterior superior temporal sulcus, medial prefrontal cortex, anterior cingulate cortex, amygdala, and other regions implicated in social functions. These brain areas are reliably engaged (more so than other areas) when we are thinking about others, interacting with them, putting ourselves in their shoes, deciding to help them, cooperating or competing with them, and so on. Basically, these are the basic elements of being human." Social pain is the experience of pain resulting from being excluded, bullied, rejected, or suffering the loss of a loved one.

I learned that similar areas of the brain that respond to physical pain are also the areas that are activated when we experience social pain. These are identified as the Dorsal Anterior Cingulate Cortex and Anterior Insula. Yet when we think of pain, we think of breaking an arm or a stabbing pain in the stomach, not of an experience when we have been socially excluded or rejected. Professor DeWall of the University of Kentucky's Psychology department explains, "Social rejection increases anger, anxiety, depression, jealousy, and sadness. It reduces performance on difficult intellectual tasks and contributes to aggression and poor impulse control." Studies show that Acetaminophen (or brand name, Tylenol) can reduce social pain just as it does physical pain. These discoveries changed how I began to view the importance of inclusion, belonging, trust, and their role in conversations.

Neuroscientist Naomi Eisenberger at UCLA designed a very simple scientific experiment called Cyberball, which demonstrated that just being left out in a game of catch, activates social pain. As more and more organizations work to engage their employees and become more inclusive, we hope that science will continue to show us how to increase the number of voices that can be heard.

"I define connection as the energy that exists between people when they feel seen, heard, and valued; when they can give and receive without judgment; and when they derive sustenance and strength from the relationship."
~ Brené Brown, Author of Dare to Lead

The Oxytocin Connection

Paul Zak, author of The Moral Molecule: How Trust Works and the director of the Center for Neuroeconomics Studies at Claremont Graduate University, was the first to identify the key role played by the neurochemical oxytocin.

He described some of his research: "A number of businesses, including retailer Zappos.com and office designer Herman Miller, agreed to let me draw blood and measure brain activity from their employees as they worked.

These tests confirmed our lab findings: Teams that caused oxytocin release in each other were more productive and innovative and enjoyed their tasks more than those whose brains did not connect to their teammates."

Cortisol to Oxytocin

When we examine how the various parts of the brain work together, the influence of being in a Cortisol flooded state is reflective of those conditions of the social brain - judging, criticizing, excluding, etc. and limits our ability to converse in an optimal manner. On the other hand, when we can regulate our cortisol and move to a more oxytocin-induced brain, we are including, sharing, appreciating, etc. We are thus more capable of empathy, connection, trust, and safety.

A Story: The Social Brain and Rejection

The social brain also triggers cortisol when our status is threatened – when we are rejected or ignored.

I had been approached for help by a CEO looking for introductions to key people in Silicon Valley. I had made some excellent connections and, at the time, was on the leadership team of an influential senior HR group. I facilitated significant introductions and ultimately secured an invitation for him to speak at a major event packed with Silicon Valley influencers.

We attended this event together. We sat together. But when he took the floor, he didn't introduce me. He didn't thank me for my contribution. He didn't mention me at all - not once during the entire evening did, he acknowledge my existence, even though I had done all the work upfront.

Needless to say, I was upset. I had been completely rejected. My status had been severely threatened. My social brain was firing, and my cortisol levels were soaring. I felt stressed.

All he had to do was say, "I am so excited, delighted that Sue has brought me to California and introduced me to such an amazing roomful of people." That would have been enough to remove any threat to my status. My cortisol levels would have remained normal. My stress levels would not have risen. And my physical and neural health would not have been in jeopardy.

Feeling included and having a sense of belonging is essential to releasing feel-good neurochemicals in the brain, such as serotonin and oxytocin.

Emotion Short Cuts

As described earlier, our brain's emotion networks are continually and rapidly scanning for environmental threats, including cues from people's faces and body language. As outlined in his book, "The Brain, from Knowing to Doing," Dr. Evian Gordon "These face and body cues convey a great deal about a person's true intentions, motivations, feelings, attitudes, and thoughts.

Authenticity and level of trust are monitored in every interpersonal interaction at every moment." By mastering and reading authentic cues, we can become aware of mismatching messages. We can act accordingly. Further, "researchers using the Total Brain Database that Dr. Gordon founded, objectively show that non-conscious emotions are constructed within the brain in a fifth of a second."

Heard and Understood

As an executive coach, the importance of Conversational Intelligence® cannot be understated. We are best equipped to help our clients with positive change when we feel heard and understood. Ann Betz, Co-founder of BEabove Leadership, describes The Seven Levels of Effectiveness in coaching and points out that "Feeling socially connected diminishes stress and can even reduce inflammation, while feeling judged or "less than" others creates fight or flight responses in the brain which inhibit learning.

When we feel we are being heard and understood, it increases the connective neural fibers in our brains - fibers that are crucial for bringing together disparate areas for increased cognitive function."

The Power of Words

Language matters as expressed by our words. In one context, words could be perceived as positive and seen as profanity or threatening in another. A great example is described by Lisa Feldman Barrett in *7 1/2 Lessons About The Brain*. "If you say something romantic to your partner who responds, "Come here and say that," your brain may predict that a kiss is in your future. If you stand up to a bully who responds, "Come here and say that," your brain may predict a threat." Which one would lead to an effective conversation or connection?

Insight - Gamma Wave Burst in the Brain

When we create the right conditions in conversation with another person, we can increase the likelihood that they will have a fresh perspective, new ideas, or insights. The state in which we experience an insight - inwardly looking, quiet, slightly positive, and not thinking about the problem, is felt when we are in the opposite of a threat state. We are open-minded, positive, and energized. These same conditions lend themselves to strong Conversational Intelligence® and effective communication.

Humor Too?

A similar activation in the brain occurs with humor, releasing a burst of gamma wave bands. As a result, we cannot be anxious and laugh simultaneously.

Mirthologist Steven M. Sultanoff, Ph.D., states, "My belief is that we are going to eventually discover that the most dramatic health benefits of humor are not in laughter, but in the cognitive and emotional management that humorous experiences provide. The experience of humor relieves emotional distress and assists in changing negative thinking patterns."

Today, research teaches us that humor decreases the stress hormones, improves the immune system, and boosts endorphins - the feel-good hormones.

Shortly after I became interested in the science of humor and its impact on health, I discovered The Association of Applied and Therapeutic Humor (AATH). Their primary mission is "...to elevate and nourish the human spirit through the intentional use of humor and laughter."

This group explains to potential new members, "we take the neuroscientific, psychological, and behavioral research of humor and show you how to use it to improve your life and the lives of others. All over the world, members are applying the strategic use of humor in countless ways. From laughter exercises for dialysis patients to training executives to use humor in leadership—even coaching people to use humor as a mindfulness strategy to decrease stress—at AATH, we're committed to making the world a happier place." What better use than in improved conversations.

I signed up for Humor Academy, a 3-year certification program that dives deeply into the holistic benefits of humor, the application of humor, and the role of humor in leadership. Upon graduating, I became a CHP, not the California Highway Patrol; it is a Certified Humor Professional. I tried to bring lightness to conversations with the clever use of words. But above all, I resolved to laugh every day as often as possible. And best of all, humor is free!

The Brain Communicating with The Heart

According to The HeartMath Institute, "When you experience stressful emotions such as frustration, anxiety, irritation, and anger, your heart-rhythm pattern becomes irregular and incoherent, negatively affecting your health, brain function, performance and sense of well-being. Conversely, when you experience renewing emotions such as appreciation, dignity, joy, and love, your heart-rhythm pattern is more ordered and coherent."

As a HeartMath Facilitator Plus, I learned more about how the brain and the heart communicate. A key measure, Heart Rate Variability (HRV), examines the variance in the time interval between your heartbeats. We want to have a more variable heart rate for great health. Thus, it measures the effectiveness of the activation of your relaxation response and the deactivation of your stress response. When optimal, it can increase coherence and deepen our connection to self and others."

Using some of their tools and apps, my clients can monitor their HRV. I love the simplicity of this program and so do my clients. It's amazing to have the ability to watch your biofeedback in real-time and then make adjustments. The beauty of it is that I can view charts and graphs and feedback showing my level of coherence. For some of my clients who have not yet embraced meditation, this approach often appeals to their data-driven thinking. As a result, they use the tools to reap the benefits.

As our knowledge of the brain and our human interactions through conversation continue to build, we will learn more about how we can shift our perspective about the brain's role in mastering conversational intelligence!

References:

Barrett, L. F. (2017). *How Emotions Are Made: The Secret Life of the Brain*. Pan Macmillan. https://lisafeldmanbarrett.com/books/how-emotions-are-made

Betz, A. (n.d.). *BEabove Leadership*. https://www.linkedin.com/in/ann-betz-a6b31018

Chang, S. W. C., PhD. (2020, March 18). *What Does "the Social Brain" Really Mean?* Psychology Today. https://www.psychologytoday.com/us/blog/the-science-connection/202003/what-does-the-social-brain-really-mean

Gordon, E. (2022). *The BRAIN from Knowing to DOING!* Franklin Publishing.

Lieberman, M. D. (2015). *Social: Why Our Brains are Wired to Connect*.

Pease, A., & Pease, B. (2001). *Why Men Don't Listen and Women Can't Read Maps: How We're Different and What to Do About It*. Harmony.

Sultanoff, S.M (n.d) *The Association of Applied and Therapeutic Humor for The Humor Academy. Total Brain mental health and brain performance self-monitoring and self-care platform*. (2022, November 14). Total Brain. https://www.totalbrain.com/

Zak, P. J. (2013). *The Moral Molecule: How Trust Works*. Penguin.

Conversing with the Elephant in the Room

~ Gwen Mitchell

"It turns out that human beings are hard-wired to have conversations that impact them in such profound and significant ways that they can actually turn genes on and off.

That's a core, fascinating challenge for all of us, and insight."
~ Judith E. Glaser

To Resilient Leaders: If you want to pivot to a more productive and efficient means of communication when addressing hot topics like fairness, inclusion, tight labor market, or woman's equality gap...what will separate your success from failure remains within your conversations.

Today's Leaders must lead with vulnerability. The recent pandemic has changed the workplace forever by shifting how work is delivered. Flexibility and adaptability in the workforce is crucial. Crashing to the surface are two interwoven initiatives: Reinventing the workplace to address the new realities while simultaneously creating fairer, more inclusive, and equitable organizations.

For Leaders, it is essential to master the power of the "We-centric conversation." Many companies do not include team input. For your company to avoid becoming a "mass resignation statistic"; experiencing significant delays in projects; or causing mistakes that result in lawsuits; your company needs to develop their C-IQ skills. The first step to mastering one's conversational power is being open to re-evaluating how you give, receive, and process information. Then the leaders can acknowledge and overcome any barriers to effective communication and accountability.

Conversations that hit the mark always address the elephant in the room. These exchanges do not happen by accident. The art of Conversational Intelligence® (C-IQ) is understanding how conversations rewire our DNA and brain chemistry.

Within this framework, Leaders gain tools to elevate the exchange of thoughts and ideas to build trust that will produce extraordinary results. Exchanges are intentional acts that require planning and consideration to connect, navigate, and grow with others. One should never forget that the primary purpose of a conversation is to give, receive, and understand the information in a way that is helpful to all parties involved.

"What" we are saying is just as important as "how" you say it. Customarily, humans tend to speak and listen with emotional attachments, which can sometimes misconstrue the message we are attempting to relay to one another. A study conducted by Stanford University shows that nine out of every ten conversations miss their mark. The real-life consequence is that 90% of the conversations that take place fail because the message gets lost in translation resulting in time lost or energy drained due to confusion and often causing hurt feelings.

Choice of words, tone of voice, body language, and timing profoundly affect the reception and interpretation of information. Like all other changes we make in our routines, business, and lives, embracing them will take time and practice.

Journey to Self-Awareness

One of the healthiest relationships you could ever have is the one you have with yourself. Learning to be honest and foster the greatness within will require sitting in discomfort long enough to recognize your patterns and their origins before rushing to fix them.

In leadership, a lack of self-awareness can be a significant handicap. A study conducted at the Northwestern Kellogg School of Management found that often, as executives climb the corporate ladder, they become more self-assured and confident. The downside is that they also can become self-absorbed and less likely to consider the perspectives of others.

To grow, one must understand what patterns help raise and/or lower your C-IQ levels. Beliefs about who we are, who others are, and how the world shapes our behavior shapes our reality. Your focus determines your reality.

During the journey, you will continuously discover what is irrelevant: that which can be stripped away to align core values with inner truths. Self-aware leaders will be prepared to facilitate others to have meaningful and productive exchanges of ideas.

Two major observations that are directly related to the full realization and utilization of this tool: Self-reflection, which is the activity of thinking about your own feelings and behavior and the reasons behind them, and Self-discovery, which is the ongoing process of stripping away that which is irrelevant, reviewing our core values, and seeking to live in greater alignment with these inner truths.

Observing Nonverbal Communication

Most experts agree that 70-90 percent of all communication between individuals is nonverbal, indicating the importance of tone of voice, body language, gestures, and facial expressions used intentionally and unintentionally to grasp a conversation's meaning entirely.

Listed are examples of nonverbal:

- Sound Effects: clearing throat, coughing, sighing, laughing, heavy breathing, voice pitch

- Body Language: shaking the head, crossing arms, tapping feet, trembling, sweating, waving, finger gesture

- Facial Expression: smiling, frowning, wincing, bulging/rolling eyes, open mouth, clenched teeth, blank stares and tears

When we think about "communicating," our thoughts immediately go to speech, but in all actuality, most ideas exchange without words. For example, when you see someone you know waving or asking a question, you respond by shrugging your shoulders. Most people use these gestures without considering how they may make someone feel. Now is the time to think about it.

Nonverbal communication helps set the mood, pace, and tone of a conversation. Leaders must be aware of the conversation beyond words to get the whole idea or message transmitted at that moment. Facial expressions, body language, and sound effects have meaning. Tapping a foot or crossing arms can carry a lot of meaning. These nonverbal cues often allude to attention spans, interest levels, and temperament.

When hitting or missing the mark in each exchange, nonverbal signals by each party support or acknowledge their position, as when someone answers "yes" while simultaneously nodding their head up-down, signaling in the affirmative.

Nonverbal cues must be observed and acknowledged since they can trigger unconscious biases that can derail a conversation if not made visible. Leaders who are oblivious to these cues displayed by the other person increase the probability of a communication breakdown.

Exploring the Cues

Unspoken rules apply whether in a professional or personal setting. During our conversations, invisible cues hide in plain sight and appear in some of the following ways: an awkward moment of deafening silence, a switch in the other person's tone, a word used that causes a chill to run up your spine, an outburst that makes hairs stand on the back of your neck, or more subtle changes in other persons physical demeanor like a blank facial expression or puzzlement in the eyes are all telltale signs.

26

When signals show up, one often makes an unconscious or conscious decision to avoid them to stop things from becoming more uncomfortable or confrontational. The problem with allowing the invisible elephants to remain in the shadows is that it creates hidden grenades that can explode at the worst time when left unattended.

Making the Invisible, Visible

C-IQ provides a way to uncover the invisible allowing for the safety of everyone involved. The first thing one should do when encountering a telltale sign is to acknowledge it by adopting a discovery mindset and asking a question to which they don't have an answer. Address the other person by name with a calm, light tone, and state... I'm observing an awkward tension in the room. Ask what the source of this tension for you is? Is it just me? If confirmed, then do what we call in C-IQ a double-click. The next step is crucial and requires you to listen to connect by seizing judgment and trying to stand in their shoes to understand their perspective. It does not require you to agree with their viewpoint but be open to the fact that their experiences may differ from yours, which makes them neither wrong nor right... just different from you.

> A conversational double-click is similar to double clicking on a computer link. You click on the link to gain access to additional information so that you can learn more. It's a deeper dive into understanding the context of a comment or an opinion that has been shared by someone else.

When we discover matters different from our experiences, it is often an excellent time to explore the story we have established for ourselves around the topic to determine if it needs to be adjusted.

Self-Assessment: The Unpacking of Your Story

When assessing yourself, determine if you are open to making changes to build healthier habits. Look for gaps in your life/practice and closely examine the rules by identifying assumptions or limiting beliefs. There are two steps in assessing yourself:

- Examine the narrative logic inherent in your current story

- Identify gaps in your narrative rationale to develop a new story

Developing a new narrative will allow you to respond to the exact situation in new ways. Given the complexity and speed of life these days, it is easy to become triggered or to accidentally provoke contrary reactions in others. When we find ourselves in an uncomfortable situation, we must remember that there is a connection between our stories, behaviors, and outcomes for which we are accountable. Over time the lines blur, and our reactions become automatic and unconscious, but we can manage them. Dr. David Drake, the founder of Narrative Coach, shares a process to pivot whenever we find ourselves in a trigger situation.

To prepare for a conversation or situation that poses a challenge, you can learn to examine your story by rewinding it.

Start by reviewing your observations about the conversation while thinking about what you tell yourself. During reflection, ask what the exchange might say about how you see yourself. Then explore "what if," consider the following:

- What was your desired outcome?

- What would you do differently?

- What shift would you want to see in yourself?

- What would you see if this was the case?

- What will you tell yourself the next time this happens?

When you rewind your story like our first author, Sue Stevenson, did with her story about the grunt, it is much easier to discover the personal growth opportunities within the experience. When you rewind and reexamine the various aspects of your situation, you can gain valuable insights. When you deconstruct your situation, you can have the opportunity to discover what really matters for each new experience.

Recognizing Your Conversational Blind Spots

Leaders must understand why they do what they do and how the stories they tell themselves and others shape their choices.

Our narrative logic, the narrative-action cycle, is comprised of blind spots: the assumptions that inform our experiences, stories, identities, behaviors, and outcomes. If not examined, it will continue to drive us in ways that may not serve us. One way to improve our Conversational Intelligence® is by recognizing and overcoming what C-IQ defines as the five most common conversation blind spots.

Blind Spot 1: "Assuming everyone thinks like me."

Assuming that others see "what we see, feel what we feel, and think what we think" is a blind spot. When we are engrossed and attached to our point of view, we cannot connect with others' perspectives.

Blind Spot 2: "Feelings don't change my reality."

This is the failure to realize that fear, trust, and distrust changes how we see and interpret reality and, therefore, how we talk about it and resolve it.

Blind Spot 3: "I can still empathize while I am in fear."

Sometimes, there is an inability to stand in each other's shoes when we are fearful or upset. We cannot imagine how another feels by our actions or their experiences.

Blind Spot 4: "I remember; therefore, I know."

This blind spot is based on the assumption that we remember what others say, rather than we remember what we think others have said.

Blind Spot 5: "I am listening, so I know what you mean."

The inherent assumption here is that meaning resides with the speaker, when meaning is actually found in the listener's interpretation of the speaker's words.

Are Blind Spots Rare?

All human beings have blind spots; it is a natural part of our human system to prevent us from losing our minds by trying to process too much data. We need to know how our minds work and what happens when driven by the I-centric impulses that lead us to conversational ignorance. Learning to step through blind spots into insight and awareness of others' perspectives strengthens our ability to create healthy environments from which trust can be established. Don't stop seeing yourself; the worst person you can be invisible to is yourself; learn to be aware of your blind spots.

A Conversation That Missed the Mark

Every conversation starts with a back story. Let's examine a conversation that missed the mark with a client we will call: Kay. The following is a look at her boss' various blind spots and what she was dealing with at work.

The leaders at her company decided it was time for a change on a mission-critical technology turnaround project. This initiative was to be the future best practice for optimizing production and delivery operations for the company while revolutionizing the industry. The team comprised a diverse group of men, each a thought leader in his respective areas of expertise.

Still, after months of missed deadlines, escalating ego confrontations, demands for additional funding, and no sign of completion, Kay could see that her company might lose their chance for creating a competitive advantage.

With a reputation for judicious use of resources and her ability to transform multi-million-dollar projects, Kay was invited to join the project in an influential "fix it" role. She was thrilled and stepped up to the challenge.

Over the first few weeks, Kay managed to deal with the lukewarm support of leadership and the team's sexist overtures, eventually aligning individual, company, and industry goals. Within six months, the team successfully delivered a working prototype that easily exceeded ALL probability or expectations. Over the next two years, the project would receive global recognition and a handsome write-up in National Geographic.

When Kay received a meeting invitation from her boss Bob, VP of Operations, to report to his office, she was excited. Her expectation was that Bob would share with Kay more information about a well-deserved promotion and salary increase.

Excited, she entered the room. As she greeted Bob with a smile, he started the conversation.

See if you can spot Bob's blind spots and which of the five examples they are:

"Kay, I want to thank you for your exemplary work on this project. I must admit I never believed you would be able to accomplish this task, especially as a woman.

You have done well for yourself, and as a black woman... your people should be proud. However, I want to be the first to inform you that we have decided to go in a different direction. We are appointing Jim as Director. We know we can count on you to support him as he takes this work to the next level. Also, I have reviewed your salary, and even though you are one of the highest-paid women in the company, I've approved a three percent increase that you can expect to see in your next paycheck. Do you have any questions?"

Stunned, she shakes her head while hearing the voice of her grandfather rush into her mind, "Words have a cost; choose wisely when you use them." Her boss' comments had missed the mark.

Kay made some decisions about her future that day that Bob would never realize were his doing. In the coming pages, we will examine an alternative approach Bob could have taken.

> Since human beings live in the why and how, Leaders must be cognizant and repeatedly ask themselves, what price are you paying for your words, attitudes, and choices?

Formulating The Recipe for Successful Conversations

In formulating the recipe for a successful conversation, it is important to determine the desired purpose for the conversation while considering the backstory that has led to the reason for the occasion. To avoid looking at the situation from one perspective, contemplate the topic from the viewpoint of everyone that will participate. What would success look like for each person? Explore how to prepare for the dialogue, set the atmosphere for it to take place, and what is happening now that others should know ahead of time so they can prepare to contribute. Just like when cooking a meal, leaders must consider all the ingredients that make up the conversation and explore where they are willing to experiment. It begins with exploring and practicing and utilizing C-IQ tools to improve how to have a successful conversation.

Managing Levels of Communications

Having a conversation with someone is like dancing with a partner. There is an ebb and flow... a synchronization that takes place as you move forward in the conversation.

C-IQ represents three basic moves which are broken into levels of conversation.

Level I: Transactional | "Telling and Asking"
This level is about passing data back and forth. Often an exchange will begin with a pleasant greeting that includes basic information about the weather. The conversational dynamics are characterized by basic telling and asking, which happens all the time and is an important part of life. This interaction includes limited emotional content.

Level II: Positional | "Advocate and Inquire"
Level II is about one person trying to influence others to their point of view. Judith describes this by illustrating two people trying to paint a wall. One person wants the wall to be green and the other orange. When one person feels inclined to try to get the wall green and pushes their agenda to make it happen. This interaction can generate positive or negative emotions for the one whose choice is not adopted.

Level III: Transformational | "Sharing and Discovering"
Judith says that transformation and co-creation take place at the point when we move into expressing Caring, Courage, and Candor.

This level is about sharing what's in your heart and discovering what is in the other person's heart without judgement. It is a sharing of concerns, fears, hopes, and desires. This type of sharing is done genuinely with an intent to get to know the other person from a place of curiosity while allowing them to also get to know you. When this level is done well, it builds trust and connection between the two brains and establishes each person as trustworthy, not a threat.

All three conversation levels are good and required for healthy communication. As one learns to perform the conversational dance, it is important to note that when moving within a conversational level, there can be a tendency for one to get stuck.

For instance, when one stays too long in Level I, sharing data they deem important, and others do not quite understand, the tendency is to escalate from telling to selling and, before long, yelling. When this happens, one's brain signals that this is not a friend but a foe. (Explore chemical conversations within Sue Stevenson's chapter)

When stuck in Level II, one is touting their position at a surface level, not sharing the internal processing that formed the opinion. We think that because we came to our view honestly, we are right and start to fight for being right, so our point of view wins the debate. Fighting for being right generates a feel-good chemical in our brains called dopamine… (for more on how the brain works refer back to Sue's chapter). Your brain can become addicted to being right, which is how and why we often act stuck.

A Level III conversation serves as a conduit to avoid getting struck and to create collaborative conversations.

Co-Creating "Win-Win" Conversations

Previously, Bob's conversation with Kay missed the mark. This next conversation helps us see how important of a role Listening to Connect plays when delivering difficult decisions. It also points out the importance of not rushing conversations, and taking the time to speak to others with compassion and from the mindset of Conversational Intelligence®.

"Hello Kay, I want to thank you for your exemplary work on this project; I admit you exceeded our expectations. I want you to know that you are a valued member of this organization.

I have a couple of items to discuss with you today: First, I would like to review the recap you provided with lessons learned for improving future projects, your career aspirations, and the next steps for this project.

Kay, you have been with us for seven years; I have confidence that you deliver when you commit to something. Have you thought about what you would like to do next?

Bob, I appreciate you asking. I want to bring your attention to one of the recommendations in my project recap report. The suggestion for a PMO center of excellence. As you know, I have volunteered on the industry - Process Improvement Practices Board for three years. I notice an emerging industry trend that correlates to successful project delivery. While networking with industry colleagues, those that have PMO centers that set and monitor project guidelines get better results. Based on additional research, I ran some preliminary numbers on our current open and set to start projects for the next two years. It looks like we can reduce delivery costs by two percent resulting in 2 million in direct cost savings within 12 months. I want to head our PMO center of excellence. What do you think?

I'm impressed. If you put together the business case, we can review it next week. Then, if everything aligns, I will float the idea at next month's regional leadership meeting.

Kay, I also want to inform you that we have decided to go in a different direction on the P&D project since you have accomplished your mission. We are appointing Jim as Director. I hope I can count on you to support him, as he has big shoes to fill.

Please understand that what I'm about to say is in no way a reflection of what we think of your efforts; as you know, with all the project overruns, salary increases are on hold this year. I can tell by the look on your face that this is not what you expected to hear; however, I secured a three percent increase in your salary at this time which you can expect in your next paycheck. Do you have any questions?"

How was the above exchange successful? Where was it not? What are three examples that support your answers?

Learn to Shift Through Changes

Change is about making someone or something different. Change has a lot to do with timing, which is often unpredictable and brings uncertainty. Resilient leaders must increase their C-IQ by learning to shift from power-over (domineering micromanagement tactics) to power-with (co-creation amongst a team) behaviors. Leaders who create "We-centric" workplaces that are inclusive of all employees and build allyships that down-regulate judgment but take the time to appreciate others' contributions to the organization, will soar to the top of "best places to work" list.

Resilient leaders that adopt a mindset of blameless discernment for themselves, others, and the circumstance give space and grace to embrace a growth culture. Focusing on expanding one's aspirations welcomes a mindset of discovery and sharing that leads to higher levels of engagement, people wanting to share their perspectives, and celebrating milestones through a sense of shared accountability.

Embracing Conversational Intelligence® as a tool for better conversations starts from a sincere desire to learn new techniques and to take the time needed to exercise these new skills. In our next chapter, Rickie Banning will talk more about successfully orchestrating change through the power of our self-talk, and how the effectiveness of our conversations starts from within each of us: It's an Inside Job.

References:

Drake, D. B. (2017). *Narrative Coaching: The Definitive Guide to Bringing New Stories to Life*. Cnc Press.

Glaser, J. E. (2016). *Conversational Intelligence: How Great Leaders Build Trust and Get Extraordinary Results*. Routledge.

Realizing It's an Inside Job

~ Rickie Banning

"The two least developed skills in the workplace are the ability to have uncomfortable conversations and to ask what-if questions."

~ Judith E. Glaser

"Ascending to the next level of leadership and leading thousands of people requires that they (leaders) be able to think like an enterprise leader. This means having one eye on the future and the other on the present. Sometimes, that eye on the present 'goes blind.' While aspiring to the next level, we fail to see what is going on right in front of us." (Glaser, Judith E. Conversational Intelligence®, p 21. (2014).

The conversation begins within ourself. It is embodied in the thoughts that we think and focus on. When we walk into the room, we bring our self-talk and invisible bias with us.

Words build worlds, as Judith says. Ensuring that we have cleared the way for Conversational Intelligence® to form can make the difference between building a bridge or building a wall within our communication with others. Realizing that it's an inside job is the first step. Let's look further and explore some of the deeper elements of C-IQ at work, shall we?

Introduction:

Throughout my life, I have held the perspective that conversations start in our own heads, that the thoughts that we think and hold in our minds not only matter but often flavor the subsequent verbal conversations that we have with others.

When we bring internal thought biases or assumptive thinking into our verbal conversations, we impact the potential outcome of those communications.

At first contact, our brain is programmed to discern friend or foe, intuitively asking, 'Is it safe, or is there danger here?'

In order to elevate our self-talk, we must eliminate our bias to hold space for conversationally intelligent communication to birth. When we feel psychologically safe in talking with another, trust is able to form and grow. In the absence of trust, our amygdala activates in flight-flight-freeze mode.

Wisdom invites us to do all we can to build a sense of safety within our communications, both with ourselves and others. Embracing key elements of C-IQ can help meet this challenge.

Curiosity Question: What biases are we bringing into each conversation?

Once we identify our biased self-talk thoughts, how can we reframe our thinking to clear the way for more effective conversations to flow?

In this chapter, we will explore 'self-talk' within the context of Conversational Intelligence® (C-IQ) and how self-talk and the thoughts we focus on can make or break the difference between an effective conversation and poor communication. I am a professional woman who takes a practitioner approach to life. In my explorations of discovery, I seek to understand, embrace, and inspire practical ways to meet problems and issues. In that spirit, as you read this chapter, metaphorically speaking, I invite you to grab an iced tea or a cup of java, sit back in your most comfortable space, and think of us as having a one-on-one conversation. I will draw examples from real-life conversations with people who used C-IQ to transform their conversations from being stuck to a place of conversational resiliency.

It is my hope that by chapter end, I will have sparked your curiosity and inspired your creativity to seek better ways of navigating communications by using the principles of Conversational Intelligence®, a transformational model of change based on neuroscience that works for everyone, from farmer to gravedigger to corporate executive, and everyone in between. C-IQ works if you work it!

> "Conversational Intelligence® is what separates those who are successful from those who are not---in business, in relationships, and even in marriages." (Glaser, Judith E. *Conversational Intelligence®, How Great Leaders Build Trust and Get Extraordinary Results* page xiii. (2014).

Pre-pandemic Comfort Zones

Once upon a time, we felt safe in our homes, communities, and living space. We didn't give a second thought to joining a large holiday crowd or even going out and about in general. Those were the 'before-times'...before the pandemic of multiple strains of coronavirus; before the massive workplace shift from in-office to remote work; before our work-life balance got turned upside down; before the ongoing mass shootings in America that are happening in our schools, our places of worship, our grocery stores, our shopping malls, in places we used to gather where we felt safe, secure, at peace.

With all of these massive changes happening at breakneck speed, with no end in sight, we as humans are being forced to step beyond our comfort zones to see our worlds with 'new eyes' and new paradigms of doing and being. The challenge before us involves communicating using more effective levels of conversations. Conversational Intelligence® (C-IQ) offers a way forward.

A Harvard Business Review article reports that according to a Mind Share Partners *2021 Mental Health at Work Report*, "Perhaps as a result of having to lead through this unprecedented era, our 2021 study showed that C-level and executive respondents were now actually more likely than others to report at least one mental health symptom."

Further, these factors heavily impacted younger workers, and members of under-represented groups, with the majority of survey respondents reporting having experienced worsening communication and a low sense of connection to or lack of support from colleagues and their manager.

Our comfort zones are being challenged daily. Meeting these challenges inside ourselves and in our daily thoughts and dialogue may hold the difference between whether we feel we are sitting in the dark or standing in the light. Finding new ways to connect and enhance our communications makes good sense at a time when we are reaching for answers to these challenges.

Pandemic Challenges: Redefining Our Worlds

The pandemic is offering us key lessons about crises, coping, and communication and is holding space for humans to redefine ourselves and our life space to support psychological safety and build trust.

In her groundbreaking book *Conversational Intelligence®, How Great Leaders Build Trust and Get Extraordinary Results,* our C-IQ mentor, Judith E. Glaser, talks throughout her book about the power of conversations that when we move conversations from the 'power-over' mindset to a 'power-with' mindset, we can bridge reality gaps between how you see things and how I see things to a higher place of trust. When trust is in the room, magic happens! We can co-create solutions and explore new ways of being.

Facing Fear and Finding Our Voice

I think that most humans around the planet would support the observation that our anxiety levels have skyrocketed post-pandemic. Many have lost their sense of physical wellness and/or psychological safety during these past few years. They are struggling to regain a sense of balance. The mental health field is experiencing epic change where so many people are seeking help that mental health professionals can hardly recruit fast enough. The telehealth industry is booming because so many folks are reaching for support to try to make sense of all these societal shifts. We are being forced to change and face our fears. Embracing new paradigms of seeing is essential to find our way forward.

As a coach, consultant, trainer, and professional psychotherapist, my professional perspective is that anxiety is a simple word for fear. My professional experience has shown that anxieties often arise when we avoid facing our feelings or deeply exploring our inner thoughts. When the amygdala part of our brain gets triggered, and we fall into flight-flight-freeze or appease mode, our brain is pumping out cortisol. This chemical causes us to feel anxious, afraid, and even down. We need our amygdala as a protective mechanism if a bear is chasing us in the woods.

Yet, we don't want our amygdala to be overworking on a regular basis, as we might be hanging out in fear-based self-talk (thoughts) or having fear-based conversations with others. When fear inhabits the room, trust disappears, and we lose our voice. As a result, we are not having the most effective conversations, either in our own heads (minds) or with others.

In order to feel better, we need to shift our brains to pumping out oxytocin. This 'feel-good' chemical takes us to the place of curiosity, creativity, and feeling emotionally safe. So, how do we do this? Keep reading!

Building Our Courage Muscle:

Learning how to build trust, create psychological safety, and build a culture of connection in our living space are key to finding our way forward to greater resiliency. Our communication with ourselves and others is a core crucible to birth inner and outer resilience.

Remember the Darwinian theory of the fittest? Those humans that embrace the challenges and commit to redefining their life space by creating new ways of connecting will be the ones to not only survive well but flourish forward into new ways of being.

So, the question is: how do I shift from feeding my fear factor to building my courage muscle? One way forward is by changing our words and thoughts from negative talk to more positive, better-feeling talk.

Louise Hay, the author of the New York Times bestseller book, *You Can Heal Your Life*, talks about the power of using affirmations as a method to reframe one's negativity into positivity. Judith E. Glaser talks about the concept of 'words build worlds.' The words we use matter, whether they are our self-talk in our own minds or the words we use with others. Using Judith's transformational model, the aim is to generate more prefrontal cortex brain activity to keep that oxytocin shower flowing and our amygdala resting. It is impossible to feel anxious and curious, and creative at the same time, as these states of being are generated by different brain center activities we think and say. This reality of how our brain responds to the power of words holds implications for all of our communications, whether in the boardroom or with our work teams and colleagues or in our community meetings and with our families and friends.

Letting Go is Hard to Do: Grieve What Was

There is an old Chinese saying: When one door closes, another opens. For us to move forward more fully into a new resilience mindset, we must do the work to close that former door. We must do our grief work around what we are letting go of.

I was fortunate to have the opportunity to study under and associate with Dr. Elisabeth Kubler-Ross. To most, she is considered to be the world's leading authority on death, dying, and managing loss. She is also known for defining the five stages of grief: denial, bargaining, anger, depression, and acceptance. We must allow ourselves, our minds, and our hearts the time and space to move through these grief stages to embrace a new resilience mindset and to reach for a new paradigm of thinking, seeing, and being.

The pandemic around the planet is a prime example and offers many opportunities for us to do our grief work. Whether that means journaling out our feelings and thoughts, expressing our emotions through sports or another momentum, sharing with a trusted friend, or seeking professional support, letting go of the old ways of seeing is necessary to hold space for our new resilience mindset. When we down-regulate fear, we up-regulate the executive brain impact, a key tenet of C-IQ.

Holding Space for Our New Resilience Mindset

So, what does holding space for our new resilience mindset mean? First, it means that we consciously accept that there is hope for creating a new vision, new eyes, and ways of seeing our worlds that might feel different yet also offer new possibilities and perspectives. Second, we are willing to trust that there is a way forward to new options as we move from self-reflection to self-discovery.

Third, how we think about those options in our self-talk and how to talk about those options in our conversations with others helps us come closer to the outcomes we are reaching for.

Embrace the New with C-IQ

I was introduced to C-IQ and Judith E. Glaser's work in late 2015. It resonated deeply. After much soul searching and lots of due diligence research, I decided to sign up to be included in Judith's first cohort of trainees to spend one year of intensive study, with Judith as our mentor, to learn her model of C-IQ. As a Baby Boomer towards the final chapters of my career, I did not take this decision lightly, both in time, energy, and fiscal investment.

Seven-plus years later, I can genuinely say that my training with Judith and my esteemed colleagues (many of whom are co-authoring this book) was the highest quality training I have had in my career, despite my having studied and earned multiple degrees and professional certifications, as a coach, consultant, trainer, and psychotherapist. C-IQ works, and I remain passionate and excited to share some practical tips for application in this chapter with you, our readers.

Two Tiny Words that Power a Giant Shift to a Broader Perspective

Words build worlds. The words we say to ourselves and to others matter. There are many articles about using effective words out there that talk about the power of saying 'thank you.' We like to feel appreciated and acknowledged; saying a simple thank you to others helps build connection and trust. That said, I would like to share two tiny words that can power a giant shift to your adopting a broader perspective. Can you guess what those two tiny words might be? Keep reading.

The power of 'yet' and 'and.' In our conversations, the words we choose matter. As Judith talks about in her book, one word can make or break the trust in the conversation.

Let us dig deeper: When we think or say 'Yes but…' that but word builds a barrier to possibility. Using the show-stopper word 'but' puts a wall up and rebuts all that came before. However, alternatively, when we choose the word 'and,' it builds a bridge and keeps the forward flow of conversation going.

Think about it. Case in point: Your direct report at work approaches you (as a boss) and says, "If I don't say so myself, I am proud of my work on that Korean client project." And you respond by saying, "Yes, you did well, 'but' your completion timeline was not what I was expecting."

Do you see how using that short word 'but' just shifted the entire communication experience toward the negative? Alternatively, we might shift to focus on the positive by saying 'Yes, you did well, and the long completion time offers a learning opportunity to identify and execute more project efficiency in the future."

Now, let's get to that short yet powerful word: **yet**. **Yet** is one of my favorite words on the planet. **Yet** holds hope and so many possibilities when we use it in our self-talk and in conversations with others.

Think about it. Case in point: Consider the word's usage yet in this example: "I may have had prior challenges learning to cook, yet this new Greek cooking class that I just enrolled in is opening up a whole new array of ethnic foods for me to work with and to try. I am excited!"

My clients that have made these two simple words a part of their self-talk and verbal conversations have reported feeling a positive shift in their communications.

It's An Inside Job: The Power of Self-Talk

Judith E. Glaser, in her C-IQ book, talks about tools and approaches such as listening to connect, not to judge or reject. The purpose of this chapter is not to review all of these; I hope you may read her book to learn more. Instead, let us review some key concepts that help form foundational ideas in C-IQ.

Listening to Connect: I do want to acknowledge how powerful setting one's intention is to decide to listen to connect.

How often have we become defensive and started crafting our next verbal retort to another without fully being present and actively listening to what s/he/they had to say? Choosing to seek to understand and listen to connect represents powerful tools in the toolkit for effective communication and conversation.

Stepping into Curiosity without Judgment: I regularly ask clients to examine their self-talk. When I do so, I always invite them to examine their self-talk without judgment and ask them to 'lean back into the hammock of you, and without judgment, step into curiosity mode; stand in your own sense of wonder, and be mindful of those self-talk messages that are renting space in your mind. See what awareness surfaces as you sit with a sense of curiosity.'

Now, the really exciting thing that I wish to share with our readers is that in every single instance where I suggest these words to a client, I observe a sense of facial relaxation move across their face. Their facial expression softens, and they visibly appear more relaxed, all because I asked them to move away from self-judgment and get curious. We loved being curious when we were young children, didn't we? Judith E. Glaser talks in her book *Conversational Intelligence®* that when we step into curiosity, we activate our prefrontal cortex, and the 'feel safe' chemical of oxytocin starts pumping. Stepping into curiosity within our conversations surely seems like a good path to follow.

In the preceding chapter, Gwen talks about blameless discernment. Ridding our self-talk of judgment is key to clearing the way to hold space for C-IQ.

To Love, To Work, To Play

Although Sigmund Freud, considered a hallmark in psychology, talked about love and work fostering our humanness, many positive psychology advocates suggest that adding in 'to love, to work, to play' is a viable adage for a balanced life. So it is from this perspective that I share the following life-relevant brief examples of how we might use the C-IQ concept of the power of words to move our conversations forward from positional and feeling stuck to forward momentum. Remember that the goal is to move from conversations that put up a wall into more elevated conversations that build a bridge forward to build a conversational connection.

I call this C-IQ from the Bedroom to the Boardroom ™ and Beyond ™ (based on the book *Conversational Intelligence®, How Great Leaders Build Trust and Get Extraordinary Results by Judith E. Glaser*)

As Gwen Mitchell discussed in her chapter, there are Three Levels of Conversation (and thinking) that are occurring as we interact with others.

Level I Thinking: Telling-Asking-Commanding and Controlling:

Case Example: To Love - Relationship

"I am a loser."

When we tell ourselves such a negative thought as this, it activates our amygdala and pumps out that cortisol chemical that causes us to feel fear and anxiety.

Try sitting for five minutes and just silently thinking this thought. Notice how your inner energy or vibration shifts downward, much like when a puppy puts its tail between its legs. That is your amygdala firing out that 'bad' chemical-cortisol.

Challenge: lack of self-loving and self-affirming thoughts, resulting in low self-esteem and confidence. The amygdala is firing out cortisol, creating fear and anxiety.

Case Example: To Work - Job and Career

"I hate my job."

Challenge: getting unstuck from negative linear positional thinking.

Case Example: To Play - Personal

"I feel trapped in this pandemic as if I cannot go anywhere!"

Challenge: Moving beyond feeling trapped in one-way thinking.

Case Example: Psychological Safety
Anxiety Facing Fear

"I don't feel safe sharing my ideas in this group."

Challenge: Moving away from fear and protection mode toward trust. Level I thinking is lockdown mode, shut-down, and closed-off circular thinking.

This next section, **Level II Thinking** explores: Inquiring-Advocating-Building Consensus-Negotiating-Compromising:

Case Example: Love-Relationship Getting Unstuck

"I am an amazing and competent woman." (or) "I am an amazing and competent man." Or "I am an amazing and competent person."

Notice now that if you sit and think this more positive, better-feeling thought for five minutes, your vibrational energy starts to shift and feel better. Your prefrontal cortex is starting to pump out that oxytocin, the 'good' chemical that helps us feel emotionally safe.

Challenge: reframing a fear-based thought and advocating towards a new, more affirming perspective.

Case Example: To Work - Job and Career Exploring New Ground

Ask yourself curiosity questions, like "What might it look like if I liked my job? How might it show up in my life if I liked my job? What would it feel like inside me to like my job? Is it possible that I may like 'some' aspects of this job? If so, which aspects? What things have I done in the past that I really liked?"

Asking ourselves these questions helps us shift from feeling stuck in one position to move toward a new vantage point.

Challenge: Moving beyond totally stuck and negative thinking that leaves you feeling drained and down; creating self-talk that yields momentum to embrace new thought paradigms.

Case Example: To Play - Personal Moving the Sandbox

"I may not be able to fly to Paris, but I can take a virtual tour of the sights!"

Challenge: transforming fear into seeing some possibility for change, moving closer to a sense of adventure by shifting positional thinking to a new vantage point.

Case Example: Psychological Safety
Anxiety Redefining a Safety Mindset

"Even though I haven't felt safe to openly talk in this group, I can reach out to one group member to float my idea and share my fears and see if s/he/they respond well."

Asking this type of question helps us move from a stuck positional place to reach for the momentum of relationship-building.

Challenge: Adopting an alternative self-talk thought that allows for positive movement and momentum towards more transparency so that trust may form.

Level III Thinking: Sharing and Discovery, Imagination, Generation, Transformation

Case Example: To Love – Relationship Co-Creating

"I am a competent woman-man-person (select whichever applies), and I will now invest my effort into creating a travel blog where travelers can take virtual tours with me!"

Challenge: Bringing a sense of adventure and new creative energy forward.

Case Example: To Work - Job and Career

Discovering Anchors and Possibility

"I commit to contacting a career coach to explore my strengths so that I may land the best-fit job for me!"

Challenge: Choosing a thought/s that invites possibility and discovery for new options; creating an action-oriented thought that helps form an anchor partnership (such as a career coach or recruiter), resulting in the formation of hope and new energy.

Case Example: To Play - Personal

Visioning Agility

"What if I reach out to friends to co-create a virtual travel group where we explore different places each month?"

Challenge: Move away from protection through positional posturing to co-creating partnering and higher levels of creativity; to move into a sense of wonder that manifests the flow of creative thought.

Case Example: Psychological Safety

Finding Psychological Safety in Our Life Space

"I realize that I have been silent a lot in our group; after reflection, I have decided to share an idea for your consideration that I am most passionate about; my hope is that you will listen to connect and explore this with me."

Challenge: Choosing a self-talk thought/s that promotes much more openness and transparency and choosing to risk trust; creating the crucible for building new trust between group members and yourself.

Resilience Mindset - The Power to Lift and Launch Momentum:

Now that we have explored a few self-talk options against the backdrop of C-IQ principles let us dive deeper into more of the tools for our C-IQ toolkit that can help us shift forward into more elevated conversations within our self-talk and with others.

Resilience Mindset Toolkit and Real-Life Stories to Support C-IQ

Here are some tools we have discussed in this chapter and/or that Judith E. Glaser endorses in her C-IQ model that helps shift from Level I to Level II to Level III conversations.

The entire C-IQ umbrella aims to shift from Level I to Level II to Level III conversations. Moving from the addicted to being right mindset and power-over, away from the protection mode, into a more psychologically safe space via our thoughts (self-talk) and the words we speak to one another requires a belief that one can get unstuck, hope that it is possible to move forward into higher ground, and partnering with ourselves (by asking positive questions that support self-affirmation) and others. This shift requires moving from defensiveness to openness, one step, one thought, and one conversation at a time. As we navigate this process, we develop what Judith calls conversational agility.

A real-life case in point that demonstrates this shift includes a time when a US Army enlisted female soldier ran up to me in the Commissary and gave me an unexpected hug, saying, "I just wanted to take the time to really thank you for opening my eyes in our Command training a few months ago on stress management and how to effectively communicate. Because you planted those seeds in our training about how we could shift our thinking and ask different types of questions to ourselves, I have turned my life around by making seven major positive changes that needed to be made. That training experience gave me the hope I needed, and your teaching us those simple techniques made all the difference. Thank you for making a living while making a difference!"

Remaining open to new ways of thinking helped this soldier change her life.

A main C-IQ concept involves accepting the premise that **words build worlds** and gaining some understanding of how the brain can be influenced by the words we think and speak. Moving our self-talk and verbal language from negative self-talk into curiosity and creativity modes helps us find inner passion, inspiration, and innovative thinking.

Consciously listening to connect, not to judge or reject, is another core principle of C-IQ. From my perspective, listening to connect truly means being in the moment and setting an intention to listen.

I am a visual learner, and I think in images, so one small self-technique I use to ensure I listen well is to imagine myself listening with 'elephant ears.' Doing this one small creative visioning process helps me truly listen to connect.

A real-life case in point demonstrating listening to connect is embodied in the following scenario. When I was first elected as International Diversity Director for a global counseling association with chapters worldwide, as part of my assuming that role, I examined all relevant aspects of their systems related to diversity. To my surprise, their fastest growing new member Chapter segment was in the international countries, outside the borders of America, where our central headquarters was located. The long-standing Diversity Committee was composed of all Caucasian males based in the USA. In all fairness, these men had helped form and develop this quality association and contributed good works to our mission, yet this, to me, who stood for inclusiveness and diversity for all, was an embarrassment. I knew what needed to be done. I also knew that I had to head off resistance to what I was about to do to gain trust from stakeholders who would, after some possible shock and consternation around fear of change, ultimately support my diverse vision for our global association.

With caring, courage, and candor, I stepped into inviting these key leaders to embrace a new paradigm of thinking. In the spirit of listening to connect, I made twelve separate lunch meetings (long lunches) with each of these respected male professionals, developing rapport, building initial connections, then starting what I knew might be a difficult conversation around our Diversity Committee and its composition and my intended changes to it. After doing lots of listening to connect, after we had some laughter and good food together, I broached the topic by sharing statistics and asking them strategically oriented curiosity questions about their vision for diversity, given that the international chapters were not at all represented on our committee. Then, I shared the tough news that I intended to balance this gap by disbanding the existing Diversity Committee by inviting others from around the globe to apply to sit on it via an application and vetting process aligned with diversity goals; that each of them was free to apply to sit on the newly formed Committee, and that only some would be selected as we needed to keep the Committee to a reasonable work group size while also ensuring that our global Chapter interests and members were being served. I then asked for their support in doing so.

It is my humble belief that these men, loyal to our association, could offer their support, despite their surprise and emotions around this change, because I took the quality time to really listen to connect with each of them. Two years down the track, after lots of hard work by our global Committee, I received a recognition award for myself and our entire Diversity Committee for the strategic changes we had made to this association, most of which are still in play today.

Taking the time to listen to connect helps build connections and those bridges of trust necessary for elevated conversations.

Double-clicking on important comments that I (in my own head) or others speak to me is another key C-IQ element. Double-clicking helps reinforce and offer support for ideas. I daresay that double-clicking can help build confidence and a bridge to a new idea by focusing on the merits of that idea or thought.

Think about how you feel when someone acknowledges something you said as worthy of double-clicking on. Just that one small action helps foster pride and self-confidence and helps build trust. I am confident that if you reflect, you can come up with many conversational examples where it felt affirming when someone double-clicked on one of your ideas or shared comments and highlighted the value of your words.

Priming for trust is another key concept throughout Judith's C-IQ model. In my working with organizational teams, if the employees or management are upset over organizational changes, then it is important to offer a safe space forum to help lead them to express their fears and anxieties about the changes, to do their griefwork in letting go of the old, so to speak, so that they may then be better able to hear about the rationale for future changes, which then helps set the stage for their beginning to talk about those changes so that eventually they come to embrace and onboard them.

A real-life case in point that demonstrates priming for trust is when I was hired as a consultant for an island nation to help the employees of the only island hospital better cope with change. The hospital hired a new CEO with good intentions and set about reorganizing the entire hospital to promote better efficiency. One of the first actions the CEO embraced was to change or tweak everyone's job descriptions and realign job roles. This action in and of itself is not a poor decision. However, one key step was inadvertently forgotten against the backdrop of successful tenets and professional wisdom on the best ways to manage change: priming trust with the staff first. By the time the hospital hired me to help them with a long-term managing change process, the entire staff was in an uproar. They were afraid, angry, and confused because no one had met with them to fully explain the intent of the changes being made and how this may impact their job futures. To make matters worse, this island hospital was the only hospital on the island, so if an employee wished to make a job change to another hospital, they had to leave their country!

I began setting about priming for trust with immediacy, with the first step in the process to introduce myself by mailing individual letters to each hospital staff, introducing the managing change project and asking each of them the same three strategically targeted questions designed to begin relationship-building before I even landed on the island, and to acknowledge their perspectives by garnering their feedback. Then, once I landed on the island, I met with all stakeholder workgroups and set aside one full day (or more if needed) to help create a safe space (without the CEO present that first day) for them to express, vent their fears and frustrations and to generally hold space for them to release their high emotions.

After all, people with high emotions cannot easily engage in critical thinking or active listening until they can express some of that high emotion. This holding space for their concerns allowed me to prime for trust in what might have been an explosive situation had things not calmed down. From there, we could then move towards higher level information-sharing and collective ideas sharing to reach a place of mutual understanding where the employees could see with new eyes the new vision that their CEO leader was moving towards.

I guided these amazing employees through Level I to Level II to Level III conversations by helping them co-create psychological safety. The process took approximately 2-3 months with 3–6-month follow-ups to ensure the internal work teams I had helped set in place were moving forward to better manage their organizational changes. None of this forward movement would have been achievable had I not primed them for trust.

Trust in relationships is the very foundation of effective conversations. Transforming the anger and fear of employees into alignment helped build ongoing trust in this organization. Leading with trust also was in play in the conversational approaches used: all embodiments of the C-IQ transformational model.

Asking curiosity questions and questions for which there are no answers (meaning formulating questions that invite the asker or recipient/s to create or co-create their own answers) is another main principle of C-IQ.

Another real-life case in point that demonstrates asking curiosity questions is well demonstrated when I attended as a Board of Directors member for a large non-profit organization. I knew that the CEO was going to raise a specific issue and likely try to steer that issue in a direction that I and others felt might be better served by a redirection. I was seen as an extrovert in this group. The group was used to me being fairly verbal about some issues or motions that came before us, so when I was purposely silent for about ¾ of this Board meeting, people noticed.

I was purposely silent because I was intently listening to connect with each person's point of view as they shared their perspectives on this issue before us; I took strategic notes and purposely coalesced the main points of all of their discussion, and at a strategic moment in time, I formulated and asked a well thought through curiosity question that literally shifted the perspectives of the majority of board members in the entire meeting, thus swaying the ultimate motion made towards the redirection. It required deep listening to everyone while balancing key stakeholder interests and formulating a curiosity question that inspired a new way of seeing. When we shift our executive brain into curiosity mode, we shift into that prefrontal cortex, where oxytocin generates.

Closing Comments-Wrap Up

In this book chapter, we have explored some key elements of the Conversational Intelligence® communication model and described various tools for achieving results that help move our conversations forward. We have talked about facing fear so that we may feed our courage muscle to have those difficult conversations.

We have talked about how conversations often begin inside our minds with 'self-talk.' We have highlighted how reframing that self-talk to ensure a bias-free mindset is important, and we have double-clicked on how erasing negative self-talk is critical to improving our conversations.

The challenges that societies face require us to come together to seek to understand, find connections and common ground and work together to see our world with 'new eyes' and a new perspective. This requires a resiliency mindset that Conversational Intelligence® embodies, teaches, and offers to those who are open to this.

 As we wrap up this chapter, I invite you to ask yourself these curiosity questions:

- What might it feel like if I replace my judgmental self-talk with thoughts that allow me to hang out in the sense of wonder?

- Where are my blind spots in this conversation?

- What might it mean for me to step out of my comfort zone and have a conversation with another person who holds the opposite world view from myself?

- What are some 'seek to understand' questions I might pose to them?

- What might it feel like to adopt a broader perspective and see the world from another person's eyes?

We are all in this together. My challenge to you is to try some C-IQ to see what emerges. An expanded vantage point can be a life-changing experience that leads to new possibilities. Let us join as discoverers and explorers as we break into conversational agility.

Launch some momentum through the power of your words!

Now let's deep dive into Susan's next chapter as she shares about how to build trust in teams.

References:

Brech, A. (n.d.). The One Unexpected Sign You May Be Gaslighting the People Around You. *Pocket*. Retrieved June 15, 2015, from https://getpocket.com/explore/item/the-one-unexpected-sign-you-may-be-gaslighting-the-people-around-you?utm_source=pocket

Deep Longevity Ltd. (2022). *Harvard Developed AI Identifies the Shortest Path to Happiness*. SciTech Daily. Note-offers a free subscription to Future Self-a free online mental health service that offers guidance based on a psychological profile assessment by AI, which identifies the most suitable ways to improve one's well-being. Credit: Fedor Galkin. Retrieved from scitechdaily.com

Glaser, J. E. (2014). *Conversational Intelligence: How Great Leaders Build Trust and Get Extraordinary Results*. Routledge.
Greenwood, K. (2021, November 15). It's a New Era for Mental Health at Work. *Harvard Business Review*. https://hbr.org/2021/10/its-a-new-era-for-mental-health-at-work

Hay, L. L. (1985). *You Can Heal Your Life*. Coleman Publishing Incorporated.

Kessler, D., & Kubler-Ross, E. (2005). *On Grief and Grieving: Finding the Meaning of Grief Through the Five Stages of Loss*. Simon and Schuster.

Knowles, D. (2022, January 15). As global temperatures continue to rise, climate anxiety will be a growing issue for young people, therapists warn. *Yahoo News*. https://news.yahoo.com/as-global-temperatures-continue-to-rise-climate-anxiety-will-be-a-growing-issue-for-young-people-therapists-warn-100035183.html?fr=sycsrp_catchall

Consulting Projects noted in the book chapter include Employee Assistance Professionals Association Intl.-Diversity Director-Committee; King Edward Memorial Hospital, Bermuda-managing change consultation; US Army-Oahu Hawaii-Command training on stress management and effective communication (2016); Unity Church of Hawaii, Oahu, Hawaii-Board of Directors meeting (2019).

Part II: Conversations: Large and Small

Successful teams begin with trust-building and intentional, masterful conversations.

In her chapter, Susan Curtin takes you through an extensive overview of the elements involved in building effective team interactions, so projects "meet their mark," as Judith would say.

You will explore Emotional Intelligence, team trust, and building the elements of Psychological Safety in teams. Very generously, Susan has included practical techniques and exercises that successful teams can use for managing the stress and challenging experiences they face.

Our final chapter features the genius of presentation skills trainer and coach Dave Underhill. Dave looks at how presenters can use Conversational Intelligence® to build trust, inspire others, and lead change.

Following the last chapter, you will find the coach-author bios. If you would like additional information about some of their work, please feel free to reach out to the authors directly or through LinkedIn.

How to Develop and Provide Trust in Teams

~ Susan Curtin

"Trust primes the pump so that people can get intimate and feel open enough to be inclusive, interactive, and intentional."

~ Judith E. Glaser

We are at a time in our world where we are facing a significant communication divide. Since the divide can be with family, friends, community members and colleagues, we may feel the strong urge to know how to rebuild connection. At the core of the rebuilding is TRUST.

Those of you who are knowledgeable of Judith E. Glaser's work and her multi-faceted dashboard, you know that at the foundation of Conversational Intelligence® is trust.

TRUST CHANGES REALITY

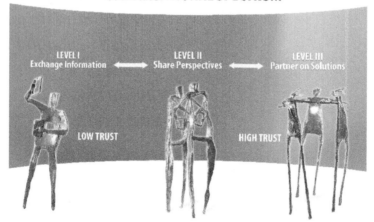

LOW TRUST	**HIGH TRUST**
Reveal less	Reveal more
Expect mistakes	Expect the unexpected
Assume the worst	Assume the best
Look with caution	Look with an open heart
Interpret with fear	Interpret with facts
Tell secrets	Tell the truth
Yes people	Yes to truth telling

On one end of the dashboard resides low trust, where individuals might show up in a self-protective mode, respond to others with resistance and skepticism. Ideally, we want to be on the opposite end of the dashboard where there is high trust, interest in partnering with others and engaging in a process of experimenting and co-creating. The dashboard offers us a means for moving forward to rebuild relationships incorporating the tools of Conversational Intelligence®.

> One definition for Trust that I have used in my programs is "A confident expectation of something". In addition, it would be the answer to the following question: "Does he/she/they have my/our best interest in mind?"

My Experiences with TRUST

When I was first introduced to the C-IQ dashboard and reflected on my own experience participating on project teams over my career, I could clearly recall experiences when there was high trust and those painful experiences when there was low trust. One project team that stands out to this day was working with a member of a project team who would bad mouth the manager to her coworkers, misrepresenting how they were being treated, while communicating with the manager in a friendly manner. Observing this behavior, I moved to a protective mode working with her, revealing less to her and was very cautious around her. She had demonstrated that she was untrustworthy and would say or do what she needed to gain approval or achieve her personal goals and ambition. Due to my low trust, I found myself resisting any of her ideas and suggestions, skeptical of her motivation, and I was not listening to connect.

> When there is low trust in a group, there are observable behaviors that include: withdrawing one's group participation, withholding one's ideas and suggestions, being more skeptical, being more guarded and defensive in communications, and dreading the time spent with those you don't trust.

Turning TRUST Issues Around

As we all know from our personal experience, we cannot make someone trust us. It is the behaviors that we each demonstrate which allows us to choose to trust each other.

So how do we build trust? What do we look for in others to give them our trust? How do we know what others need to feel the level of trust needed for partnering?

We know that Trust is the foundation for all successful relationships, the critical question we need to ask ourselves is *"How are we creating trust in our relationships and what do we know about others need for giving us the trust we are seeking?"*

The following are two questions that I ask in my coaching programs. They provide the opportunity for self-reflection by answering questions and identifying what team members currently are doing and what they might do differently moving forward.

1. In your Trust Circle, who would you let into the circle, and why?

2. Who would you not let in and why?

There has been much written and discussed on the importance of trust, if we all know that it is so important, what is getting in the way of our achieving it? Therein lies the challenge, to know, to understand, and to do. I interpret true learning as "Knowing, Doing & Being". Knowing trust is important but if we are not demonstrating the behavior in our Doing then we don't transform into Being who we want and how we want to engage in the world and seen as trustworthy.

Take a moment to reflect and answer the following questions:

- Which personal behaviors, actions, and attitudes do I use to *build trust* with my family, friends, employees, co-workers, and clients?
- Which behaviors, actions, and attitudes have I found that *disrupt trust* with my family, friends, employees, co-workers, and clients?

In response to your answers provided, consider what you might do or say or think (self-talk) differently going forward. As a reminder of what was covered in Rickie's earlier chapter on the internal conversations, reflect on your current mindset, actions, and words you will be more intentional in using on your self-growth journey.

To establish a foundation of trust on teams, we can prime our conversations by using the 5 Step model Judith created. The 5 Steps allow for closing reality gaps and opening up views that will elevate the conversations on the team.

Step 1: **T**ransparency - Quelling Threats and Fears

Step 2: **R**elationship - Listen to Connect

Step 3: **U**nderstanding - Listen to Understand

Step 4: **S**hared Success - Listen to co-create Strategies for Mutual Success

Step 5: **T**est Assumptions & Tell the Truth - Listen to Close the Reality Gaps

"Conversations are multidimensional, not linear. What we think, what we say, what we mean, what others hear, and how we feel about it afterward are the key dimensions behind Conversational Intelligence®."

~ Judith E. Glaser

TRUST on TEAMS

*Lencioni, Patrick M.
The FIVE Dysfunctions of a Team: A Leadership Fable. Wiley 2010

In Patrick Lencioni's Five Behaviors of a Cohesive Team program, **Trust** is the foundation of the Five Behaviors Model and the building block to achieving team success. If you don't have Trust, team members will be unwilling to engage in constructive conflict, fall short on committing to the projects, and don't hold each other accountable. Each of these key steps ultimately influences the team's ability to achieve results.

> **A definition for Trust: The Five Behaviors of a Cohesive Team:** "Confidence among team members that their peers' intentions are good, and that there is no reason to be protective or careful around the group."

In essence, teammates must get comfortable **being vulnerable** with one another. Creating trust requires developing vulnerability-based trust. This requires us to know one another personally to successfully work together professionally. Getting to know others more personally utilizes the Conversational Intelligence® skills of Listening to Connect, Asking Questions for which you don't have the answers, Double Clicking to gain deeper meaning of what is being communicated and staying curious to discover more about the problem and the individual. These C-IQ skills were also referenced in Gwen and Rickie's chapters, and you will see them again in the chapters that follow.

Here is how I put it into practice:

I recently worked with a team where one member of the team had filed a complaint against the leader, resulting in the CEO requiring coaching for the leader and a teambuilding session for all the team. It was apparent at the first teambuilding session the individual who filed the complaint had low trust. He showed up to the session defensive, resistant and skeptical. He was disengaged, worked on his computer, and continued having side bar conversations with a team member who sat next to him. His table was behind the leader and other managers, so he was able to hide his behavior and stay disengaged.

On Day 2 the seating arrangement was changed requiring his full participation. Since everyone was actively participating, he learned that he too needed to join in and share his responses. As the morning progressed and he felt heard and seen by others he became less guarded and more trusting of the process. The exercise on vulnerability-based trust, where members learned more personal information about each other shifted his energy and focus to being more open and curious. He actively participated in the activities that allowed other team members to better understand his behavioral style and motivations.

What could have turned into a very stressful environment for the leader transformed into a learning opportunity that permanently and powerfully shifted the level of trust in the team moving forward.

"You must trust and believe in people
or life becomes impossible."
~ Anton Chekhov

Psychological Safety as a Key Ingredient

Amy C. Edmondson, Novartis Professor of Leadership at the Harvard Business School was the person who first introduced the construct of "team psychological safety". Her area of expertise is leadership, teaming, and organizational learning. She had pursued research on what creates a learning organization, initially focusing on teams in healthcare organizations. It was during that early research that she discovered the importance of team psychological safety, defined as "a shared belief held by members of a team that the team is safe for interpersonal risk taking".

Dr. Edmondson's further describes psychological safety as a climate that one believes you can speak up, a sense of permission for candor and that your voice is welcomed and a belief you have been heard. It is not about being comfortable, it is the willingness to challenge, the courage to share, including what you don't know, and the willingness to be vulnerable. The skill set required to create the climate include calling attention to the challenge, asking good questions and listening. The skill set represents the Conversational Intelligence® tools of asking questions that you truly do not have the answers, double clicking to gain deeper meaning and understanding, and listening to connect so individuals truly feel heard.

Google's Project Aristotle, combed through decades of academic research about teams and then scrutinized and surveyed teams at Google over a period of years. Psychological Safety turned out to be the underpinning of those identified as high performing. More than anything else, a sense of psychological safety, or a shared belief that the team is a safe place for interpersonal risk-taking, was critical for making the team function effectively.

"There's no team without trust," says Paul Santagata, Head of Industry at Google. Addressing Paul's observation that there is no team without trust, then knowing how to build that trust would mean incorporating CI-Q into your trust-building activities.

So, let's explore the main ingredients of creating a psychologically safe environment.

Psychological Safety is present when we thrive in environments that respect us and allow us to (1) **feel included**: the need to be accepted precedes the need to be heard. (2) **feel safe to learn:** learner safety satisfies the basic human need to learn and grow. (3) **feel safe to contribute**: allowing us to co-create with others (Level III conversations), and (4) **feel safe to challenge the status quo:** ability to give and receive feedback.

If we don't feel or have these basic foundations, it is emotionally expensive and fear shuts us down. We find ourselves experiencing low trust and possibly engaging in the work with greater resistance and skepticism. We're not happy and we're not reaching our full potential as individuals or as a team.

To participate in Level III Conversations we must enter them with openness, curiosity, and the possibility of transformation. When the environment nurtures psychological safety, there's an explosion of confidence, engagement, and performance.

> *"In good conversations, we know where we stand others; we feel safe."*
> *~ Judith E. Glaser*

 Ask yourself if you feel included, safe to learn, safe to contribute, and safe to challenge the status quo on teams that you are a member.

Finally, ask yourself if you're contributing to an environment where others can do these four things: 1) Feel included, 2) Feel safe to learn, 3) Feel safe to contribute and 4) Feel safe to challenge the status quo.

When there are work cultures of Trust, leaders and team members demonstrate the following trust behaviors: transparency, vulnerability, authenticity, honesty, the capacity to listen deeply especially to perspectives different from their own.

"Curiosity is more important than knowledge."
~ Albert Einstein

Creating Safety

For creating Psychological Safety and to feel safe to challenge the status quo, it requires us to build our capacity to provide feedback and receive feedback from others. The second ingredient of learner safety also requires our ability to give and receive feedback, ask questions, experiment, and risk making mistakes.

These two ingredients require the use of the Conversational Intelligence® skills: Priming for Trust, Asking Questions for which you don't have the answers, Listening to Connect, Sustaining Conversational agility to Refocus, Reframe and Redirect.

Mindset Matters

Having a growth mindset and staying curious allows us to grow from the feedback we receive from others. We need to trust that the feedback is being provided with our best interest at heart. Our ability to give and receive feedback is a critical communication and vulnerability skill as well as an important aspect of providing Psychological Safety for others.

Often, without recognizing it, we struggle with our own stereotypes and misperceptions about other people – our "lens" or the filters present in our thinking.

The following are two models I have created: one for preparing to deliver feedback, (the BEAM Model[©]) and the second, (the GLOW Feedback Model©), for using to ensure you are skillful in giving and receiving feedback. Both are elements of the Managing4Results™ Program.

The BEAM Model© is an Emotional Intelligence process /tool that helps us understand the origin of our ideas and how we filter data and our experiences, often in very narrow or limited ("myopic") ways, which limits our success.

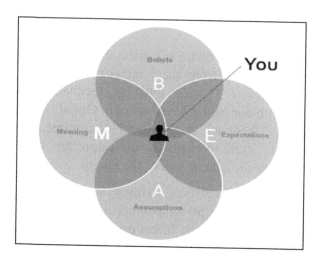

BELIEFS - We filter what we see and experience in the world through the lens of our beliefs.
EXPECTATIONS - Based upon our beliefs, we will have expectations of what we want or need as an outcome in any situation.
ASSUMPTIONS - When our expectations are not met, we often assume why things happened without verifying the validity.
MEANING - Out of the assumptions, we give meaning to the experience that often reinforces our original beliefs' if we don't question them.

*Managing4Results™ Program

The model is dynamic and interconnected with the goal of asking questions to uncover one's current beliefs, expectations, assumptions, and meaning of the world or others. The circles overlap with one another, and the center circle represents you. Like an orchestra, each aspect affects the other; if one changes, the others change. Even the person as a whole can change because BEAM is a way of shining light on what might be hidden or unknown.

BEAM Model© Exercise

There is abundant research in psychology and written on workplace learning theories that substantiate the theory that people with high self-efficacy get ahead better, communicate and assess situations better than those with low self-efficacy.

Instructions: This is a fill-in-the-blank exercise for low self-confidence (self-efficacy) issues. Self-efficacy is the belief that we will get positive outcomes through our actions.

The task: Providing feedback to an underperforming individual. Below are reflective questions for your consideration:

- Think of a time when you worked with someone you had to provide feedback or someone you might know currently who was underperforming,

- Review your beliefs, expectations, assumptions, and meaning for why they might be underperforming.

- Put yourself in their shoes as someone who does not think they have the skill to take on additional assignments.

- What logical expectations and assumptions would this person hold in their head? What if there were facts contrary to their assumptions?

- Work through the BEAM Model in preparation for providing future feedback.

Beliefs	Expectations	Assumptions	Meanings
I am not as capable as most people to take on additional work assignments.	If I accept the additional assignment, I could fail to deliver.	If I fail to deliver on the assignment, I could lose my job.	I can't afford to lose my job, so it is best that I don't accept any additional work assignements.
Beliefs What are your current beliefs regarding their ability & performance?	**Expectations** What do you expect will be the outcome of providing them with feedback?	**Assumptions** What assumptions might you be making about the individual or how they will receive the feedback?	**Meanings** What meaning might you be assigning to their current performance issues?
Productivity			
Attitude			
Communication			
Capability			

Once you are clear about your Beliefs, Expectations, Assumptions and the Meaning you are holding, you can confidently move forward with delivering your feedback to the person intended. The GLOW model provides you an approach for providing the feedback and in receiving any feedback from the individual because ideally, feedback will flow in both directions.

The Glow Model

The Glow Model is a tool to help you become skillful in giving and receiving feedback from others.

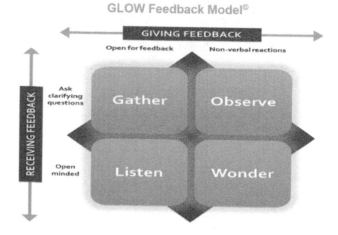

GLOW Feedback Model©

Gather	When **giving** feedback first gather information to confirm that the person is interested and ready to receive the feedback and ask clarifying questions if you are receiving the feedback.
Listen	**Giving** feedback requires you to listen to any clarifying questions asked of you. In receiving feedback, you must listen with an open mind and accept the feedback is true from their perspective.
Observe	When **giving** feedback you want to pay attention to how the person is receiving the information, observing their non-verbal reactions, and asking clarifying questions to confirm their understanding. **Receiving** feedback, you also want to observe & manage your own non-verbal communication.
Wonder	When **giving** feedback be curious about your own expectations and motivations in sharing the feedback. When **receiving** feedback be curious on how the information shared could possibly be shining light on some personal blind spots.

*Managing4ResultsTM Program

100

The following is an example of using the GLOW model© with a client who was seeking feedback from their team on how to strengthen communication and trust.

Seven Steps to The Feedback/Feedforward Process

1st – Identify your key stakeholders to seek their input.

2nd – Connect with them and share you are working on your Leadership Development Plan and would appreciate their feedback/feedforward focusing on what matters most to them.

3rd – Send them the three questions you would like their input prior to meeting with them in person.

4th – Schedule the meetings with each of them to learn about their responses, prepared with asking clarifying questions and a curious mindset.

5th – In the meeting, begin by thanking them for their willingness to share their perspective.

6th – In your meeting with them ask only open ended and clarifying questions starting with What or How and questions that you do not have the answers.

7th – In closing, thank them for their time and feedback and let them know you will be following up with them to share your plan and continue to ask for their feedback/feedforward on their observations of any changes.

Suggested Questions

- What are one or two things I can begin doing to be a more effective leader?

- What are one or two things I can begin doing to be a more effective communicator?

- What are one or two things I can begin doing to build greater trust?

- Anything else you would like to add?

Client Insights

The outcome of receiving their feedback, she was able to listen with an open mind and accepted the feedback was true from their perspective. She asked only clarifying questions and questions she did not have the answers.

She was able to observe & manage her own non-verbal communication, knowing her brain was experiencing the conversation as a threat state.

While receiving their feedback, she stayed curious about how the information shared could possibly be shining light on some personal blind spots in her communications and trust building.

She was able to identify specific behaviors and mindsets she wanted to change moving forward to strengthen her communication and trust with the team.

Giving Feedback

- First review your personal beliefs, expectations, assumptions & meaning about the issue (BEAM).

- Prime for Trust.

- Use "I" statements.

- Focus on behaviors and actions, not attitude or personality.

- Be specific with behavioral examples in the areas for growth.

- Be descriptive rather than evaluative.

- Focus on what you want, not what you don't want.

- Constructive, Constructive, Constructive

- Check feedback accuracy and veracity.

- Deliver with tact, respect, and consideration.

- Ask them if they have any questions or need for clarification.

- Thank the person for being open to the feedback.

Managing4Results™ Program

Receiving Feedback

- Keep an open mind.

- Use active listening skills, paraphrasing when necessary.

- Accept the feedback as true for the person delivering it.

- Ask questions for what you don't have the answers.

- Listen to Connect.

- Don't get defensive if you disagree with the feedback.

- Respond only to clarify and/or ask for specific behavioral examples.

- Double Click on words to deepen your learning.

- Look for the opportunity to learn from the feedback, take what you need and leave the rest.

- Resist justifying your actions or behavior.

- Thank them for their willingness to share their feedback with you.

"If you only do things, you know well and do comfortably, you'll never reach your higher goals."
~ Linda Tsao Yan

A Precursor to Psychological Safety: Building Your Conversational and Emotional Intelligence

In Tasha Erich's five-year research program on self-awareness, the researchers discovered that although 95% of people think they're self-aware, less than 15% actually are. In a cross-industry survey of working adults, 99% reported working with at least one unaware person, and nearly 50% worked with at least four. Peers were the most frequent offenders with 73% of respondents reporting at least one unaware peer, followed by direct reports (33%), bosses (32%) and clients (16%).

I believe the outcome of this research speaks directly to what gets in the way of providing or experiencing Psychological Safety. These numbers point to a need for the development of self-awareness in team members, managers, and leaders. Self-awareness helps people more effectively collaborate and communicate at work and build trust and Psychological Safety. Being self-aware, I need to know when I am communicating with someone in a Level I, II, or III conversation.

~

Next, we will look at five simple ways to increase your Conversational and Emotional Intelligence that will help build trust in your relationships.

CONVERSATIONAL SPECTRUM MATRIX

CONVERSATION LEVELS	Level I	Level II	Level III
PURPOSE	Exchange Information	Share Perspectives	Partner on Solutions
BEHAVIORS	Tell & Ask	Advocate & Inquire	Share & Discover
MINDSET	Resist/Doubt	Doubt/Disengage	Explore/Collaborate
TRUST LEVEL	Low Trust	Selective Trust	High Trust

Connection Across Behavioral Styles

We normally communicate with others in a behavioral style that is most comfortable for us, and we don't normally consider our audience as often as we could. If someone shares our style, we might connect sooner and engage with greater ease. For example, as an extrovert I often engage in conversation and build off other extroverts' thoughts and ideas quickly. If I use that same behavioral approach with an introverted colleague, I might shut them down or potentially cut them off and lose out on their input and perspective. I first need to be aware of my natural communication style, then observe the style of my colleague, then figure out how to adapt and engage with them effectively. I may need to pause more with my introverted colleague, ask more open-ended questions, listen more, and allow them the reflective time they need in conversation.

As a leader, adapting across behavioral styles is even more important. Expecting your employees to adapt to you, with the power differential, can lead to disengagement, low trust and missed opportunities.

Perspective Taking

We often enter conversations aware of only our own perspective. We can be quick to share what we think, feel, or believe about the issue or situation. Even if we are self-aware, we also need to be aware of the other person's thoughts, feelings, and experience. Observe their body language and how what you said landed with them. Ask them what they think. Look for and try to understand their perspective. This is particularly important in today's virtual environment. Managing relationships well requires us to enter conversations with an open mind, open ears, curiosity, and without judgment. First seek to understand and then discern.

In both Gwen and Rickie's chapters they discussed the need to be aware of bias and to reduce judgment. Judgment builds walls which shut down trust. In case of Conversational Intelligence, the goal is to build our capacity for blameless discernment and to increase our capacity for non-judgmental perspective taking.

Knowing Your Negative Triggers

A negative trigger is an emotional reaction that can shut down access to our prefrontal brain with negative results. In a triggered state we are most likely operating from our amygdala or reptilian brain. We can lose perspective and might find ourselves more defensive, judgmental, or avoidant. Communication can break down and relationships can be damaged.

Be conscious of what triggers negative responses in you. If someone says something that you perceive as offensive or disrespectful, how do you respond? Do you take it personally? What feelings and emotions show up? How do you behave in the moment? Do you shut down, get angry, or say something that you may regret later?

 We need to be aware of our triggers so we can take steps to respond more effectively in the moment.

Mindfulness Practices

Experiencing a negative trigger often causes an amygdala hijack, when our amygdala takes over and we are more reactive, losing access to our Executive brain used for calm, clear headed decision making. Sue referenced Physical Threats and Neurochemistry in her earlier chapter.

We react unconsciously; our breathing is shorter, our muscles are tighter, our pulse rate more rapid. Common responses are fight-flight-freeze or appease. The key is to intercept the hijacking by shifting your attention.

Using a Conversational Intelligence® technique, we could respond with a "Pattern Interrupt" because once we recognize we are triggered, we need to make a shift. We can reframe our attention by focusing away from any negative self-talk. Self-talk can be uplifting or become a saboteur; our inner conversations are something we can monitor.

An effective way to focus away from the situation is to reframe and refocus our thoughts and subsequent reactions. Some techniques that make that possible are to monitor our breathing, or to create an intentional physical sensation such as rubbing two fingers together to redirect our focus.

Each time we catch ourselves in an emotionally triggered state and choose to shift our focus, it allows us to build new neural pathways. These new neural pathways result in greater clarity, calm, and curiosity, which aid us in making better connections in our relationships.

Technique One: Deep Breathing

The simple technique of deep breathing is available to you wherever you go and allows for shifting attention. Try breathing in deeply for a count of 5, pausing for 2, then breathing out for a count of 5. Repeating this several times will shift your focus and brain chemistry resulting in more clarity and calm.

While you pay attention to your breath, focus on a positive feeling or emotion. This helps you reset, giving you the time to shift out of the negative reaction and accessing the calmer, clearer, resourceful parts of your brain. Now you can choose to respond more mindfully, to listen better, to empathize more, and to explore alternate responses resulting in greater confidence and trust in the relationship.

Technique Two: Constructed Emotion Creation

Dr. Lisa Feldman Barrett's research and theory of constructed emotion can also shed light on Trust and Psychological Safety. Her model outlines how the brain constructs emotion. She speaks to how our brains are "meaning making" and "predicting" all the time, and often making prediction errors. What happens next is the story we tell ourselves about the person or situation resulting in less trust, less openness, and reduced transparency.

The fact that our brain is guessing and creating meaning from stimuli arriving from our senses and past experiences, and using those prior experiences to respond and create meaning about what others might be feeling, can limit us and impact the quality of how we respond to others and to uncertainty.

Since our brains are constantly predicting, and most likely experiencing many prediction errors in our interpretations, C-IQ teaches us about "Pattern Interrupt" as a technique for slowing down our misaligned responses.

When we can remove the prediction errors related to old interpretations, beliefs, narratives, we can create quality conversations. To find out more about pattern interrupts, you can also reference NLP (neurolinguistic programming) for more background on this technique.

In the next chapter, Dave Underhill will dive deeper into the work he is doing to show leaders how to develop their impact, and to inspire and influence others within their respective organizations. We will see that at the heart of their business transformations is an intentional focus on creating amazing business outcomes through the power of Conversational Intelligence®.

References:

Barrett, L. F. (2017a). *How Emotions are Made: The Secret Life of the Brain.* Harper Paperbacks.

Eurich, T. (2018, January 4). What Self-Awareness Really Is (and How to Cultivate It). *Harvard Business Review.* https://hbr.org/2018/01/what-self-awareness-really-is-and-how-to-cultivate-it

Delizonna, L. (2017, August 24). High-Performing Teams Need Psychological Safety: Here's How to Create It. *Harvard Business Review.* https://hbr.org/2017/08/high-performing-teams-need-psychological-safety-heres-how-to-create-it

Glaser, J. E. (2016). *Conversational Intelligence: How Great Leaders Build Trust and Get Extraordinary Results.* Routledge.

Lencioni, P. (2010). *The FIVE Dysfunctions Of A Team.* John Wiley & Sons. *The Five Behaviors of a Cohesive Team.* John Wiley & Sons, INC. 2014

Rainey, C. (n.d.). *HR Leaders.* https://hrleaders.co/podcast

Rozoysky, J. (2015, November 17). High-Performing Teams Need Psychological Safety: Here's How to Create It. *Re:Work.* https://rework.withgoogle.com/blog/five-keys-to-a-successful-google-team/

Conversations that Build Trust and Inspire Change

~ Dave Underhill

"Trust is the glue that holds an organization together in the face of enormous challenges."
~ Judith E. Glaser

"Every voice counts. Make room for them."
~ Dave Underhill

The scope and speed of change we're experiencing creates pressure for leaders throughout their organizations. Executives search for ways to rebuild trust within their companies in the midst of a 'great resignation'. Managers struggle to connect with teams working in a variety of hybrid environments. Everyone faces challenges building relationships with an ever-changing list of leaders, peers, employees, and other stakeholders.

Why is this important? A recent survey by Gallup indicated that when followers strongly agree that they trust their leaders they are four times more likely to be engaged than when they don't find leaders trustworthy!

In previous chapters, Sue, Gwen, Rickie, and Susan shared their insights on how Conversational Intelligence® (C-IQ) is a valuable tool that leaders can use to guide themselves and others through these challenging times. In this chapter, I'm going to focus on how leaders can use C-IQ to engage people in large conversations such as presentations and group meetings, as well as in their smaller 1:1 interaction.

Why Conversational Intelligence®?

I believe that every voice counts. For the past 30 years I've helped leaders find their voice so they could deliver presentations that engage and inspire their audiences. In January 2016, as I listened to Judith deliver a webinar on C-IQ, I realized that the concepts she was sharing around neuroscience, trust, and engagement were going to be critical to leaders delivering presentations.

The more I learned about C-IQ, the more I wanted to build it into how I coached leaders. To that end, I signed up for both the virtual training and a six-month coaching certification process. It was during this certification process that I met my esteemed colleagues. We developed an immediate rapport around C-IQ and years later, we continue with our commitment to use the concepts to grow in our professional and personal lives. It's an honor to work with them on this book and an honor to share my ideas with you.

My goal in this chapter is to show how you can use Conversational Intelligence® to present your ideas, engage others, and use your voice to positively shift difficult situations. I love stories, so in this chapter I'm going to take you on a journey of how one leader, Charles Simmons, used C-IQ to lead his organization through a transformation in how they created results and conducted their business.

The Leader

Charles Simmons is the Chief Technology Officer (CTO) of a large, multinational financial services company. He joined the company in 2019, just before the pandemic, and has been on a roller coaster ever since. Despite the economic disruption, the company has grown the number of employees by 25% and instituted a work-from-home policy that has dramatically changed how people interact. I was coaching Charles on his leadership communication.

As we discussed his goals for coaching, he worried about how he was going to get people to commit to a multi-year transformation in how the company used technology to serve its customers.

"We've grown so fast that I feel I don't know half the people in my organization. They certainly don't know me. Many of them are still growing into their roles and learning how to navigate our culture, at a time when we're making changes in how we work. We need them to quickly grasp why we're doing this massive transformation and how they are key to making it happen."

While Charles was known as an executive who delivers results, he had a sense that he would need a new set of skills to succeed on this project. He needed to use every presentation, meeting, and conversation to build a deeper connection with people.

Building Trust and Engagement

Leaders are constantly talking about change. They ask people to support company strategies, adopt new policies and procedures, and change behaviors to adapt to a 'new normal'. The level of trust the audience feels around the change impacts their engagement with it. That trust level is influenced by many factors: the nature and scale of the change; their confidence in their ability to change; and their perception of the risks and rewards involved.

As Sue and Susan mentioned in their chapters, when people experience low trust or threat, they're likely to resist, be skeptical of change, or just wait and see what happens. As trust increases, they experience more psychological safety and are willing to try out new ideas and collaborate on solutions. This connection between trust and engagement is a key concept in Conversational Intelligence®.

The following Conversational Spectrum provides a framework for understanding people's state of mind and how it impacts the way individuals engage with any kind of change. Leaders can use this framework to understand their audience at a deeper level by exploring the following questions.

CONVERSATIONAL SPECTRUM

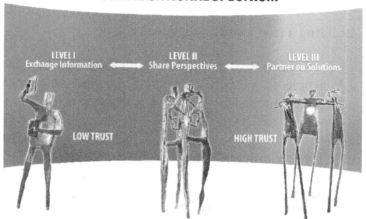

- What is the trust and engagement profile for this group? Evenly distributed? Concentrated in one area? Split at each end of the Spectrum? Why is that - what biases and points of view do they have about the change?

- What issues and concerns need to be addressed for people to feel a higher level of trust and engagement? What Levels of Conversation fit the situation?

- What goals and motivations do people have that would lead them to embrace change?

- What are the best ways to communicate and connect with people? Large/small group sessions? 1:1 conversation? Virtual or in person?

Gaining these insights helps leaders select the information and approach that builds trust with each audience.

The All-Hands Meeting

The first chance Charles had to present to his entire organization about the technology transformation was during his manager's all-hands meeting. We used the Conversational Spectrum as the starting point for planning what he wanted to say. His key insight was:

"I think most people are disengaged, in a wait-and-see mode. This is the first time they've seen the full plan for the transformation and I'm sure they are uncertain about how it will impact them. They also don't know much about me and my background, so their trust in me as leader is unknown. An unspoken dynamic with this group, The Elephant in the Room, is that people are already stressed out in their jobs, so if they start feeling overwhelmed by all the changes, we're taking a risk that they'll quit. We need to hit the right note with this presentation."

With this background, we decided that the overall goal for the presentation was to shift people's engagement from wait-and-see to exploration and active involvement. The benefits of this shift would be reinforced in discussions during team meetings following the town hall.

Charles had 50 minutes total, spread throughout the town hall. With the active involvement goal in mind, his plan was to:

- Share the Why behind the transformation. How customer feedback and competitive pressures were driving the change.
- Co-present with members of his leadership team around organizational goals, strategies, and roles/responsibilities for the change.
- Share a short story of his experience with large transformations and empathize with people's concerns ("I know it can seem overwhelming at times... In my first leadership role I...")
- Show how the organization plans to support them with tools and other resources during the transformation effort.

The feedback on the town hall was very positive. People felt more informed and confident about the direction the company was heading. Charles recognized the need to repeat this type of communication over and over as the transition rolls out. His biggest insights were around his own role:

"I enjoyed telling the story of my background, and I got positive comments from people on email. I need to do more of this to gain their trust. Let people know who I am, what I believe in, and what my vision is for the organization. I need to get to know them better as well."

The question was, how?

What did Charles do in the all-hands meeting to build trust and engagement in his organization?

What can you do more of in your presentations, meetings, and conversations?

The Trust Factor

One of the big casualties of the recent pandemic and economic disruption was trust. Trust in organizations, between co-workers, and even trust that the future will be better than today have all been impacted. Once trust is lost, it takes a long time and sustained effort to rebuild it. Employees look at how leaders behave to gauge how committed the organization is to creating trust.

Recent studies identified empathy, transparency and listening as leadership traits that build trust. Other surveys found that 68% of CEO's believe that showing empathy will lead to a lack of respect. It's clear that many leaders are uncomfortable demonstrating these soft skills, to the detriment of their effectiveness and their organization's success. As Judith mentions in Conversational Intelligence®, employees want more than just business-speak from leaders, they want a deeper connection with them.

There are ways for leaders to put trust at the forefront of how they approach conversations. Here are four steps you can take to set up your communication for success:

1. Be open about your goals and concerns. As Susan mentioned in her chapter, this level of transparency helps to establish psychological safety for others to be open and honest.

2. Plan for how you can establish a culture of collaboration where inclusion and engagement are a key element of creating solutions.

3. Step into each other's shoes so you discover and see multiple perspectives on the impact of change.

4. Take time to create a shared picture of success. What does it look like to all parties? Invite others to share their ideas.

When leaders approach their presentations, meetings, and conversations with a trust mindset they create an environment where other people are open to sharing ideas. With added trust, people are more committed to the success of the organization.

Getting to Know You

Charles didn't need to wait long to find an opportunity to tell more stories. A few weeks after the Town Hall, the company's HR department reached out to him to see if he'd be interested in participating in their new "Getting to Know..." leadership series. In these one-hour sessions, leaders

---

from different parts of the organization would meet with 40-50 employees and respond to questions, so people could get to know the leader better. Charles said yes.

While he was excited about doing the Getting to Know interviews, Charles was also quite nervous.

"Even though I've been in leadership positions for many years, I'm more of an introvert. I don't usually share much personal information about myself but know it's important to do as a leader."

As we discussed this perception, he had of himself, he realized that his self-talk held him back from advancing in his career and that he did have valuable insights to share.

The good news was the HR department sent him a list of questions they ask every leader, as well as audience questions that had come up in other sessions. The list included topics such as:

- Tell us about your career journey and how did it lead you to your current role?

- What does work/life quality look like for you and how do you manage your work-life quality?

- In your opinion, what are the biggest challenges facing leaders these days?

As we practiced the questions, we used the idea of building trust to craft responses and tell stories, so people got to know him better. We focused on being open and honest when responding to the HR questions. In preparing for audience questions, the emphasis was on connecting with people.

The session went quite well – people on the call told Charles that the stories he told gave them a better sense of who he was personally and as a leader. He decided to use the Getting to Know format with other groups as a way to help people understand him and each other.

He also realized that he needed to have trust and relationship-building conversations with his own leadership team.

 What stories can you share with others to help people know you better?

In what ways might you make it comfortable for other people to tell their stories?

Letting Go, To Grow

One of the most difficult transitions for leaders is to make the shift from doing to leading. In his best-selling book What Got You Here Won't Get You There, executive coach Marshall Goldsmith lists "Adding too much value" and "Not listening" as two of the twenty bad habits that keep leaders from becoming more successful.

Adding too much value is a common behavior among leaders and subject matter experts who can't seem to step aside and let other people learn how to solve problems. They'll tell people what the solution is, micro-manage their employees' progress and even jump in to work on the problem if things don't go the way they think they should. When they do this, leaders are definitely not taking time to ask questions or listen to input from others.

While leaders may feel they are helping, their employees see these behaviors as disrespectful of their abilities and a sign that the leader doesn't trust them with the work. This lack of trust has a negative impact on motivation, engagement, and productivity.

As Rickie wrote in her chapter, sometimes leaders need to let go of beliefs and unproductive behaviors to make room for new ways to have conversations. One new skill that leaders can embrace from Conversational Intelligence® is Listening to Connect. It comes from practice and setting up conversations as a two-way street.

Building Trust One Conversation at a Time

Charles took a lot of pride in the technical expertise he'd built throughout his career. He was recruited into his current position based on his track record in delivering breakthrough technologies and exceptional business results. He attributed his success in large part to this knowledge and his hands-on approach to getting things done.

While Charles experienced success after joining the company, as he took on more responsibility, he started feeling that he couldn't effectively manage everything that was on his plate. His perception was confirmed by an employee survey where people made comments such as "He needs to trust his people more", "Delegate more work", and "Take time to connect with people".

As we reviewed the survey, he acknowledged the comments:

"I agree with what they are saying. I've been such a hands-on problem solver in my past roles that it's hard to change, though I have to delegate more if we're going to accomplish our goals. I can't do it all and I really want to work at a more strategic level."

Being a hands-on leader, Charles' next step was to put a delegation plan together.

A key element in Charles' approach was his view that delegation was a shared task. It wasn't a one-and-done meeting where he gave people a list of new things to do. It was a series of conversations, and coaching, which would be tailored to each person's situation.

He started with two people on his leadership team who were ready for advancement, made a list of responsibilities that he needed to hand off, and drafted a delegation and development plan for each leader. Next, he outlined what he wanted to cover in the conversations and how to make it a collaborative effort. Like Gwen outlined in her chapters about levels of conversation, he wanted to talk about delegation from a variety of perspectives. He would:

- Take time to understand their personal situations, motivations, and ambitions. How could he help them realize their goals and dreams?
- Discuss how they contribute to the organization's success.
- Show appreciation for their work and for their commitment to growing in their role.
- Share mutual expectations around accountability, measuring progress and timing of meetings.

He felt this approach would create a sense of psychological safety and allow them to talk about the details of the tasks and the big picture around the leader's goals and motivations.

It took a while for Charles to see the impact of his delegation conversations. Everyone was incredibly busy, and he found that sticking to a regular schedule of 1:1 meetings and coaching made a difference.

His proof came one day when one of the leaders on his team told him how much she appreciated how he spent time and effort connecting with her at a personal level. It helped her better understand him as a leader. She also valued how he delegated more and provided support when she asked for it.

What ideas do you have about how Charles could improve his delegation conversations?

What would you want to talk about if you had a delegation conversation with your manager?

How to Succeed with Conversations, Large and Small

The scope and speed of change are only going to increase as we move deeper into the 21st century. This makes it even more important that leaders have skills in Conversational Intelligence® that will help them to build trust and engage people in solving the challenges they will be facing together.

To wrap up, here are a few thoughts on how to succeed in your conversations.

- Be Curious. Understand your audience's state of mind. What's their level of trust and engagement?

- Focus on What Matters. Identify what each audience needs to know and feel to increase their level of trust.

- Listen. Make your communication a two-way street, so people get a chance to share their ideas.

- Embrace the Journey. Building trust takes time and may include multiple conversations. Use those conversations to learn and grow.

"A single conversation across the table with a wise person is worth a month's study of books."
~ Chinese Proverb

References:

2021 State of Workplace Empathy: Summary Report. (2016). In *businessolver.com*. https://businessolver.com/workplace-empathy/

Glaser, J. E. (2014). *Conversational Intelligence: How Great Leaders Build Trust and Get Extraordinary Results*. Routledge.

Goldsmith, M., & Reiter, M. (2007). *What Got You Here Won't Get You There: How Successful People Become Even More Successful*. Hyperion.

Gallup, Inc. (2023, February 13). *Develop leaders and managers at all levels - Gallup*. Gallup.com. https://www.gallup.com/workplace/216209/develop-managers-leaders.aspx

The 13 Behaviors Of High Trust Leaders. (2022). The 13 Behaviors of High Trust Leaders. https://resources.franklincovey.com/the-speed-of-trust/the-13-behaviors-of-high-trust

C-IQ Coach-Author Profiles

The C-IQ West Coast Mastermind consists of seven certified graduates of Judith E. Glaser's first Conversational Intelligence®® classes in 2016.

The mastermind grew out of a three-person San Diego C-IQ study group consisting of executive coaches who had worked together on various San Diego engagements. Susan Curtin, Sue Stevenson, and Timi Gleason were all enrolled in the first Conversational Intelligence® training that formally began in January 2016.

Hawaii-based Rickie Banning later became part of their study group. Then, during the nine-month coaching certification phases, three more members: Gwen Mitchell (Texas), Dave Underhill (Oregon) and Tim Warkentin (Canada), joined to form a certification cohort.

Early on, Judith turned to the West Coast Mastermind for feedback and dialogue. Additionally, members of the Mastermind have contributed behind the scenes to develop and catalogue content, and to define the various iterations of C-IQ materials. They have served on marketing projects, as student mentors, group facilitators, and subject matter experts for the classes that followed.

From the beginning, Judith envisioned a legacy that could be passed on and embraced through her students. It is with great honor that we share her work, and it is to our delight that you have chosen to join us.

Rickie Banning

 Coach 'Rickie' has 40+ years of experience as a global organizational consultant, coach, and corporate trainer, in engagements in all regions USA and Puerto Rico, Australia, Bermuda, Canada, Japan, and the UK. Known to her colleagues as 'strategy in motion,' Rickie offers a warm, practical approach to individual, team, and organizational clients in specialties including change management, crisis response, cultural diversity, management momentum, team building, and workplace bullying prevention.

Since 2017 C-IQ Certification, Rickie has worked with the Defense, Federal, non-profit and private sectors to help management leaders and employees improve effectiveness by drawing upon the key principles of Conversational Intelligence®.

Rickie has earned certifications in Human Resources Management and Employee Assistance Programs and is a licensed psychotherapist. She is an award-winner for developing the violence prevention program for the largest organization in America, Rickie uses a systems approach to help people discover practical solutions.

Reach Rickie: Rickie@coachmomentum.org

Susan Curtin

Susan is an award-winning organization development professional and has been an Executive Coach for over 24 years. She assists with issues around employee engagement, leadership development, and team building. In 2008, Susan founded a leadership, talent, and succession management consulting firm: Insights4Results, which is a California based LLC corporation. For information about programs and services see: www.Insights4Results.com.

Susan has created and licensed Managing4Results™, a successful, comprehensive management training that incorporates the development of a department manager's role as a coach for ongoing employee engagement and increased retention. This program teaches all managers: "How to be, What to do and When to do" to build stronger relationships with their direct reports through giving constructive feedback, coaching, and communicating in ways that truly motivate and enable teams to achieve greater results.

Susan is a Board-Certified Executive Coach; EMCC Global Senior Practitioner; and has a Master Corporate and Executive Coaching designation. She is an alumnus of the first Conversational Intelligence®® Certification program and incorporates the C-IQ tools & techniques into her coaching and organization development practice.

Reach Susan: Susan@insights4results.com

Timi Gleason

Timi was fortunate to work with Judith before she passed away. They co-created and won a bid together to provide C-IQ to a global med-tech firm. Delivering content for a winning bid with Judith is an experience that Timi will always treasure.

Timi is an Executive Coach for leaders of global teams. Her emphasis is on strategic thinking, communications, and executive presence. Conversational Intelligence®® is a teaching tool that helps her clients overcome struggles to work together. Timi is also the 2021 creator of Soulwork Maps®, a unique destiny-path tool that combines birthday numerology and two popular and time-tested leadership assessments. Website: soulworkmaps.com

For our C-IQ book with six authors, we needed a book shepherd to oversee the combining of six unique voices and areas of expertise. Timi has provided the connecting content between the chapters; created the structure for the contributors; and has overseen the layout and flow so that all the content has continuity.

Timi has a Bachelor of Sciences degree; certifications in Systems Thinking, Creativity, Strategic Management and Commercial Design. She is an Amazon author: Becoming Strategic: Leading with Focus & Inspiration.

Reach Timi: StrategyCoach@executivegoals.com

Gwen Mitchell

 Gwen serves as the visionary founder and managing partner of 3rd I Business Solutions. Additionally, she is a certified Global Team Coach Practitioner, motivational speaker, and author. Her mission is to provide businesses with the structure needed to empower performance excellence, bringing clarity to the chaos.

She is known for being A Change Coach: promoting changes in the way you think, listen, speak, problem solve, and do business: changes that not only affect the corporate bottom line but also how you conduct yourself in life. The goal is to evolve into the best version of "you."

The cornerstone of her process is communication – she utilizes the principles of Conversational Intelligence® to create safe environments for all voices, an inclusive feeling, and to develop and improve critical listening skills. By implementing her proven techniques, people who work for the same entity become team players with a united goal of working in unison for the company's overall success.

Reach Gwen: Gwen@3rdiprocessfx.com

Sue Stevenson

 Sue is the founder of Lifted Fog, a global executive coaching practice. She facilitates learning and positive change utilizing the latest research in neuroscience, Conversational Intelligence®®, brain health, and strategic humor management to help leaders realize their full potential and success.

As an author, Sue's book "Impossible to Possible: Neurostrategies for Healing, Humor and a Reimagined Life" offers hope and neurostrategies to executive women who feel burned out or in need of a new way forward. Sue has been published in Success is a State of Mind and co-authored a White paper, "Humor and Coaching," with Karyn Buxman.

Currently residing in Southern California, Sue loves golf, tennis, pickleball, and photography. She is energized by living around water and is best known to be "an engaging conversationalist, a broadcaster of happiness, and a fun-loving and spirited storyteller with a wee bit of Scottish humor that makes her a delight to know."

Reach Sue: suestevenson13@gmail.com

Dave Underhill

 Dave Underhill believes that every voice counts. As a presentation skills trainer and coach, Dave helps leaders find their voice and communicate in ways that build cultures of trust, partnership, and innovation.

Since founding Underhill Training in 1993, Dave has worked globally with companies such as Microsoft, Intel, Genentech, eBay, SAP/Concur, NIKE, Silicon Valley Bank, Callan Associates, Polen Capital, CFA Institute, TA Realty, Oregon Metro and Fred Hutchinson Cancer Center. He's also coached hundreds of entrepreneurs on their investor presentations through his work with the Oregon Venture Fund, The Indus Entrepreneurs (T.I.E.), and Portland Seed Fund.

Dave has a BS from Oregon State University and an MBA from the University of Washington. He received his Conversational Intelligence® certification in 2016. He is a regular yoga practitioner, bikes, swims, and enjoys living in the Great Pacific Northwest with his wife, Dixie, and daughter Emma.

Reach Dave: daveu@underhilltraining.com

Chas Martin - Artist

 Chas Martin lives by three basic questions: What if? What else? Why not? This incessant curiosity is the foundation of his creativity.

After studying Visual Communication at Pratt Institute in New York City, Chas worked with Boston and San Francisco ad agencies as an art director and creative director. He honed his visual skills creating ads, TV commercials, package designs and exhibits. Exploring different startups during the early dot com days, he became an expert at PowerPoint for investor presentations. He turned invisible concepts into credible imagery.

He turned to fine art around 2008 and has worked primarily as a sculptor since 2015. Unlike 2-dimensional media, his sculpture has a theatrical relationship with space. He uses that space to create suspense and engage viewers.

Chas is a former instructor at Boston Art Institute, San Francisco Academy of Art University, Pacific Northwest College of Art, Northwest Academy and Sitka Center for Art and Ecology. He lives in Portland, Oregon. His imagination, however, is not geographically attached. Chas's sculptures and masks are in collections in Europe, Africa and throughout the U.S.

Reach Chas: Chas@ChasMartin.com